HENNING CHRISTIANSEN

BJØRN NØRGAARD

MANRESA HAUPTBAHNHOF

An Homage to Joseph Beuys and Ignatius of Loyola

1994

In the 1960s Fluxus movement, Joseph Beuys found the possibility to broaden the older concept of art based on artistic disciplines, to the point that, following the dynamic of life, he was able to encompass any human activity: art = life. The flux of materials, the principle of heat as an energy activator, along with copper, felt, fat, honey and lead, amongst other materials of symbolic substance, gave the artist an individual mythology for the transformation of the individual through a self-determination process, resultantly transforming the social fabric.

In various actions from that period, he would stage initiation journeys or pilgrimages to holy places and others with special cultural and symbolic energy. In the action MANRESA (Galerie Schmela, Düsseldorf, 15/12/1966), Joseph Beuys unites a place with its symbolic value. In the script for the action he writes, 'Auch zu dir fliege ich, MANRESA' (I am flying to you too, MANRESA), taking a city as the hot spot of a spiritual geography and transformational, reparative energy. Saint Ignatius of Loyola, wounded in battle and converted into a pilgrim, laid out the theoretical and practical foundations of what would be his transformational army of souls in the *Spiritual Exercises*, which he wrote in Manresa during his stay in 1522–1523, illuminated by the period he spent on the sacred mountain of Montserrat. Here is where Beuys encountered a biographical parallel with his own life: the crash of his military plane on the Crimean front in 1943; his injuries and physical pain; and a therapeutic way to heal contemporary man. For Beuys, the action MANRESA opened the doors for social sculpture, posing the question 'Where is Element 3?', which can only be answered by each individual.

In this 1966 action, Joseph Beuys was joined by the composer Henning Christiansen and the sculptor Bjørn Nørgaard, two Danish artists who broadened the action Beuys had conceived with resources from their own creative languages, intervening as well in the script, which was signed by all three. The message: the split of contemporary man, the halved cross that man with his efforts must complete, between reason and intuition, between mysticism and politics, in a double movement from North to South and East to West, in the continent known as Eurasia. This is how one of the scores of the action MANRESA, entitled *N/S/E/O* (1966), situates a European cross with Manresa (light) and Rome (classicism) in the south, while to the north there is Copenhagen, a point even further to the north where Manresa's light and intuition and Rome's classicism find their way, and which Beuys places at the Thorvaldsen Museum.

After Beuys's death, a new MANRESA action led by Henning Christiansen was held at the Kunst-Station Sankt Peter in Cologne, on 21 February 1991, on the occasion of the 500th anniversary of the birth of Ignatius of Loyola. On 4 November 1994, the two Danish artists, like two pilgrims, arrived at the town of Manresa to expand the message of the original Beuys action. If in 1966 the action rendered homage to Alfred and Monika Schmela, the action *Manresa Hbf* had Joseph Beuys and Ignatius of Loyola as its subject. In *Manresa Hbf* (1994), the incantation comes full circle. The two artists travel with a suitcase, which symbolically carries within it the travelling pilgrim (*Der Reisende*) and the wounded man (*Der Verwundete*), in reference to Beuys and Loyola. Together with other tools employed, the invocation of the 1966 action is completed, coming to fruition with the energy of the site. Beuys sees Manresa as a *Braunraum*, a brown space of substance, in a mystical geography where in 1627 the Christ of Tort, a sculptural relief in a mystical mandorla, a medallion from the wayside cross now at the Saint Ignatius Cave, would sweat blood. The counter-space to this would be the Thorvaldsen Museum in Copenhagen.

The action *Manresa Hbf*, which was attended by a thousand people, had as its main participants Henning Christiansen and Bjørn Nørgaard, with Christophe Charles on sound, Friedhelm Mennekes participating in the action and Harald Szeemann offering a lecture to present the exhibition of the same title, which featured drawings, scores and pictures of the town of Manresa. The action was carried out over six stations in Ignatian spaces along the River Cardener, and took the name *Manresa, Central Station*, referring to a symbolic site where the transformation of the individual might be possible. 'Mysteries take place at the central station, and not at the Goetheanum,' Joseph Beuys once said to a journalist, in a declaration where he distanced himself from the anthroposophy of Rudolf Steiner while drawing nearer to sites of work and movement: a train station, a factory, and so on. Indeed, the action begins in Manresa's Guia shrine, which looks down onto a train station.

This volume brings together for the first time the unpublished material from the action MANRESA (1991) and the action *Manresa Hbf* (1994): drawings, scores, photographs, texts and the full script of the latter action. Friedhelm Mennekes, who was a witness to and unique participant in these actions, as well as being a researcher into the relationship between Joseph Beuys and Ignatius of Loyola, provides a detailed description of the six steps or stations of the action *Manresa*

Hbf and its symbolic meaning in relation to the original 1966 action. He observes that the notion of 'Manresa' for Beuys and Loyola was a 'terra sancta' on both a psychological and topographical level, while also being a model for persistent disciplined action, something which has enabled Beuys's collaborators to broaden his message beyond his death in 1986.

In my particular case, I expand upon the meaning of the European cross that Beuys drew, and the values of the southern Manresa. I point to the principles that move Joseph Beuys's work and action, such as those of heat, evolution and power, all of which are present in the posthumous development of the action MANRESA (1966), along with the memory of the original action, his two close collaborators' transmission of it and the Manresa the place as *Braunraum* (Brown Space), which finds its counter-space at the Thorvaldsen Museum.

Peter van der Meijden, an expert in the work of the Scandinavians Henning Christiansen (1932–2008) and Bjørn Nørgaard (1947), addresses Christiansen's collaborations with Beuys before 1966 and the impact of their actions on Nørgaard, who was then a young art student and sculptor. He further discusses the action MANRESA (1966), the long period from 1967 to 1994 and the action *Manresa Hbf* (1994). Van der Meijden's text deals with the dialogue, methods and narrative of both artists as applied in the 1966 action, in cooperation with Beuys: transformation, illumination, responsibility and social change. This analysis is founded on the text by Henning Christiansen entitled 'Reality Multiplied by Three: Four Epistles on Joseph Beuys's Working Methods' (1968), which is also published in this volume. The text speaks of reconciliation of opposites: space and 'counter-space', time and 'counter-time', as well as the concepts of 'action', 'demonstration', material reality, psyche and poetics in Beuys.

Finally, in his lecture for the inauguration of the exhibition *Manresa Hauptbahnhof* in the Sala Plana de l'Om in Manresa, Harald Szeemann speaks to the profound interest in man as grounded in the sculpture of Beuys, after the experience of this artist at the Kassel documenta, a text which has not been available until now.

This book has been published on the occasion of the 500th anniversary of the period Ignatius of Loyola spent in Manresa, along with the volume entitled *Joseph Beuys – MANRESA: A Spiritual Geography* (2021).

Pilar Parcerisas, Editor

Scores by Henning Christiansen for the action *Manresa '91*, which took place at Kunst-Station Sankt Peter, Cologne, on 21 February 1991, and were later used for the 1994 action.

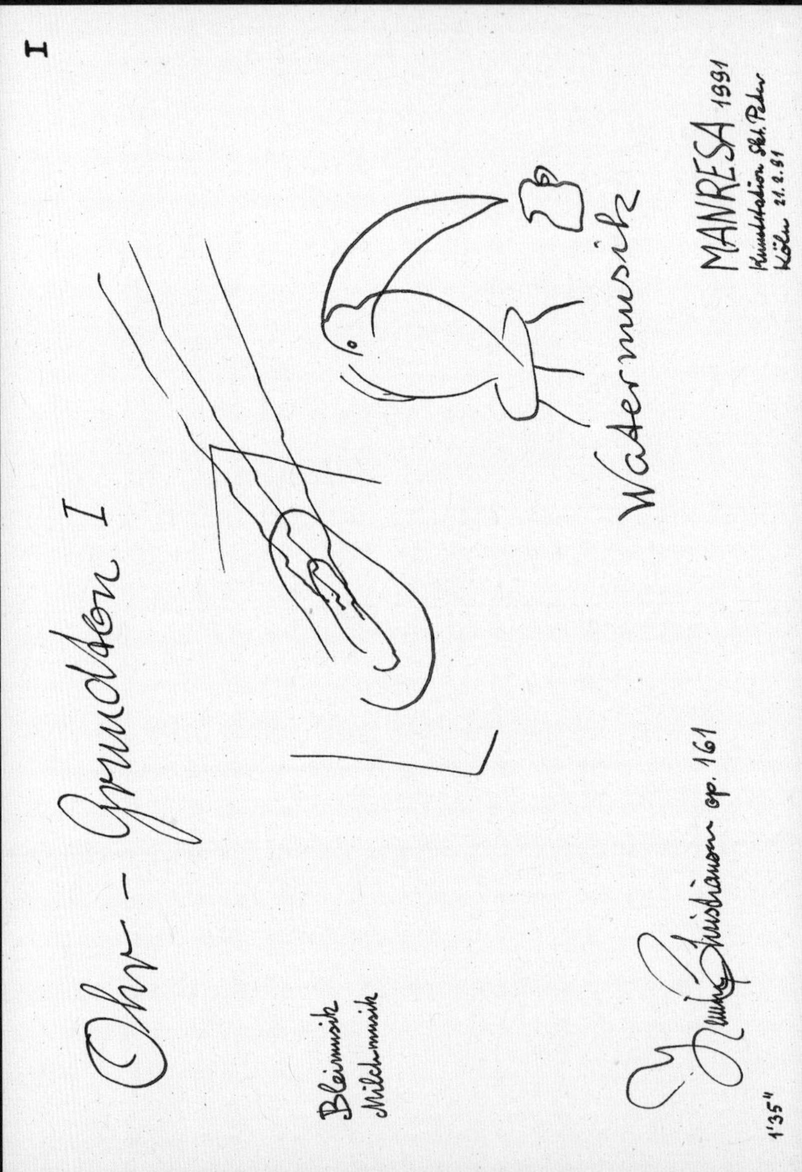

Ear - Basic Tone I

Lead music
Milk music

1'35"

Henning Christiansen op. 161

Water Music

MANRESA 1991
Kunst-Station Skt. Peter
Cologne 21/2/91

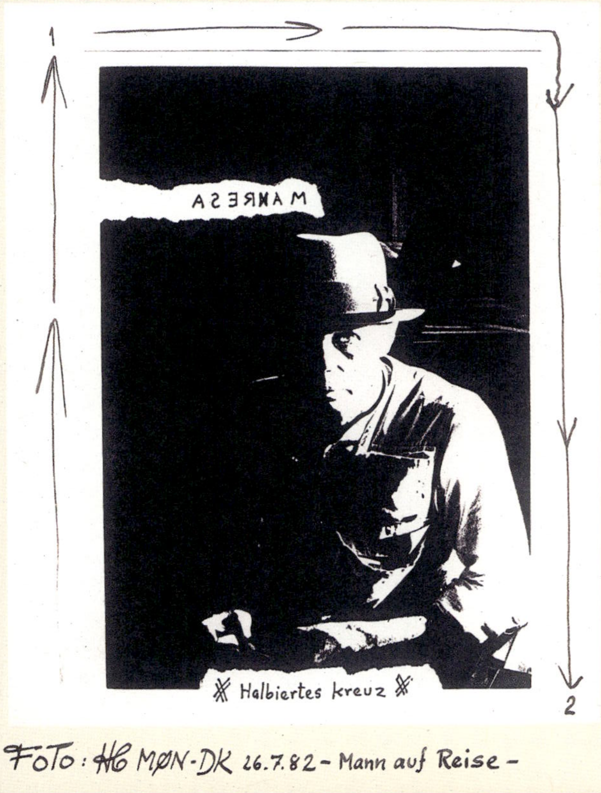

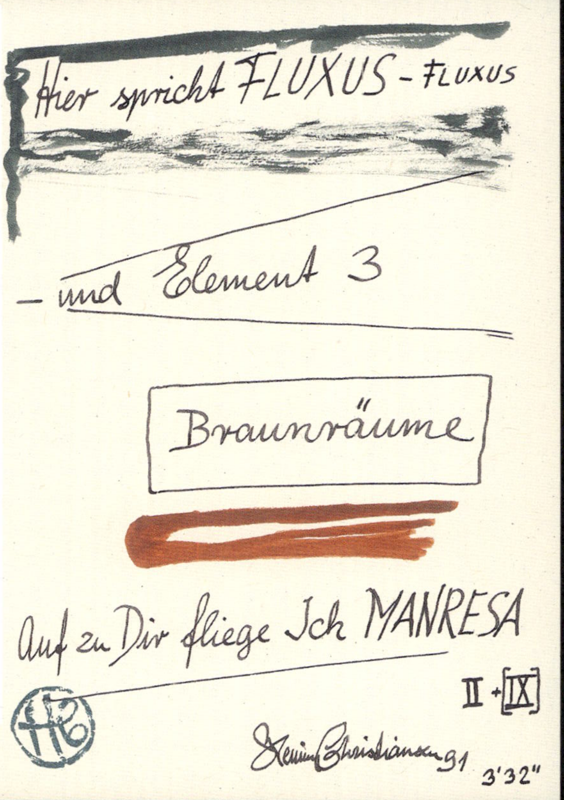

This is FLUXUS speaking - FLUXUS

and Element 3

Brown Spaces

I am flying to you too, MANRESA

II+[IX]

Halved cross
PHOTO: HC MØN-DK 26/7/82 -Travelling man-

Henning Christiansen 91
3'32"

with halved cross

Columns of sound

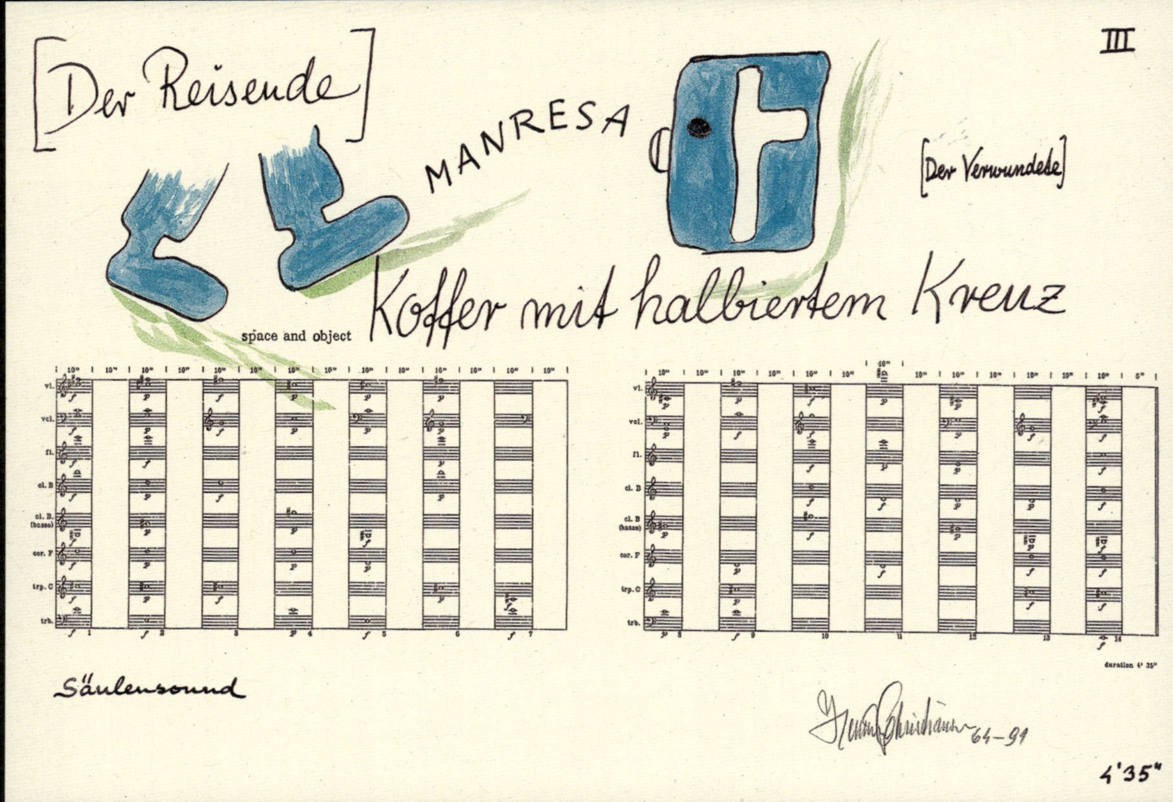

Henning Christiansen 64-91

4'35"

Dialectical Evolution Ib (Arithmetik)

IV

11111
77777
111111
222222
1111111
44444
11111111
777777
2222222
33333
22222222
55555
222222222
7777777
444444
555555
66666
5555555
2222222222
666666
111111111
4444444
6666666
333333
77777777
44444444
3333333
22222222222
1111111111

444444444
55555555
222222222222
555555555
66666666
33333333
5555555555
4444444444
777777777
2222222222222
666666666
11111111111
6666666666
333333333
44444444444
3333333333
22222222222222

Counting-Song

3'50"

Henning Christiansen op. 16

1963

Counting-Song
3'50"

Henning Christiansen op. 16
1963

Time

reading...

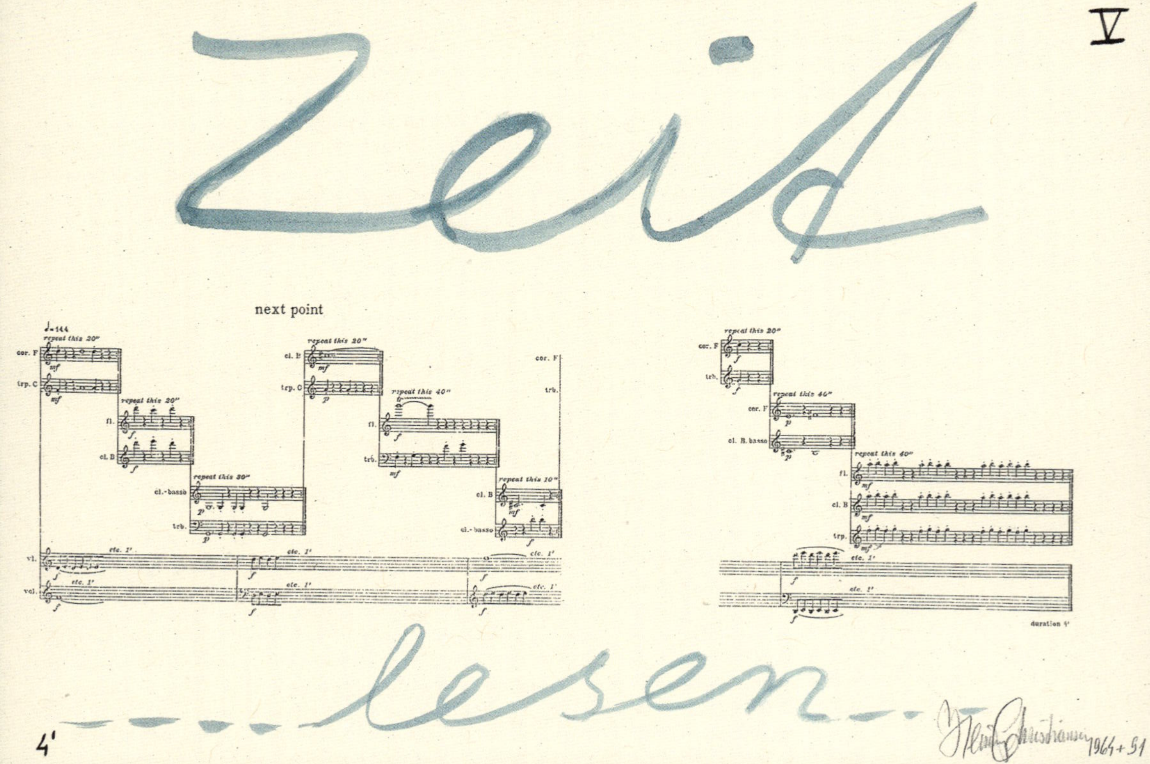

TIME. "time stood still" — you can write — you can say. But it can't Time never stands still, like a quiet river it glides into silence. It doesn't care about what we have or haven't done. It is inexorable and tells only that: nothing is eternal, not even the earth on which you stand. Or the rock you are holding in your hand. Call time unswerving, it isn't that it goes on and just goes together with you, as long as you can follow You can't hear it, but you can measure it and turn it into action, but that is work of man, time doesn't care about that. You have to make it ring, only we can make it visible — for some time. Go on — go on — therefore you can assert, that time is the most important element of music — of film — of all "ephemeral" arts — the ephemeral arts thrive on it, they devour time. Though you can hear music in your own head – you can only condense it. Even when you are reading, time devours you, but it fills you with something else, which you can hurl back into the face of time, when it allows you to digest what you have read. You are a "victim of the course of time" and "you have to know the time of your visit", that goes for politics, that goes for war, that goes for everyday life. "time is money" is a saying, and everyone tries to concretize it, but time doesn't care about that. Let time pass, it does anyway, you could suggest, but that is not possible, because time demands, it burns energy. It almost seems as though it needs you, but it doesn't. Time is inevitable for people, irresistible. It seems that earth too is influenced by time, but it only seems so, because seen from a time's perspective it isn't! The earth turns by order of time. The world of the human race turns — the human conception of the world turns — and we call it evolution. It is somehow, but from time's perspective it isn't. While time turns the world, — we stand and wonder, no matter how fast we run or how much we shoot. Time is so installed in each individual, that he participates in it, but without influence on time's course. What time is it — is it what time — time is it what? — time doesn't turn, it stands still and moves. It doesn't grow. It is invisible. But it needs energy from the universe. As the world turns, we turn. Time lives off the energy of the whole and we are forced to supply time with the necessary energy. War is the worst enemy of time, it uses up too much energy and not enough remains for thinking, after time has gotten its share. Man remains dull and lost. But time doesn't care, it goes on — on and on — it stands solid and quiet and moves, as if nothing happened.

As the world turns, we turn. But time doesn't care, inexorable.

Henning Christiansen, Jan. 91

Manresa - 15/12/66 - 21/2/91

can't - (...)

plaster feet

of
Bjørn Nørgaard 66

(ikke=not) (can - can't)

Manresa - 15.12.66 - 21.2.91 VI

ikke kann - kann ikke - kann kann ikke ikke -
kann ikke kann - ikke ikke ikke kann kann kann -
kann ikke kann -
ikke ikke ikke ikke kann kann kann kann ikke ikke ikke kann -
kann ikke kann -
ikke kann ikke kann ikke kann kann.

von
Bjørn Nørgaard 66

(ikke = nicht) (can - can't) dauer: 1'30"

Worte: Hans-Jörgen Nielsen. Behandlung: Henning Christiansen

Duration: 1'30"
Words: Hans-Jorgen Nielsen. Performance: Henning Christiansen

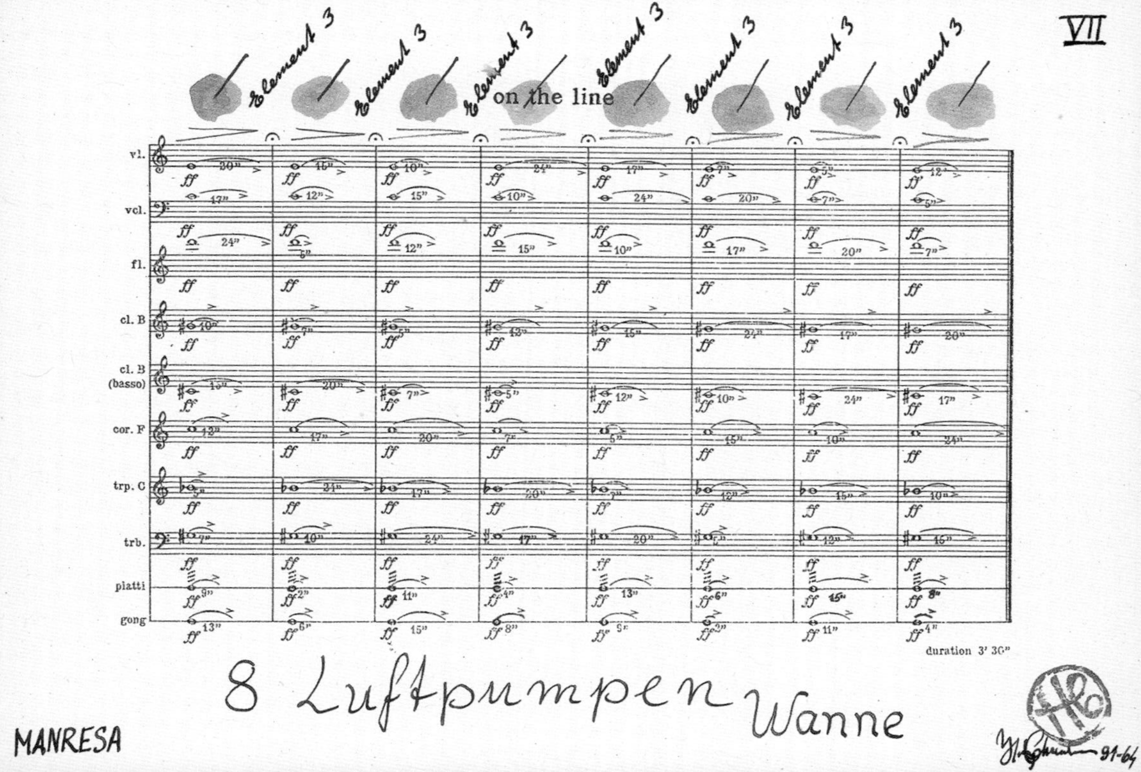

MANRESA 8 bicycle pumps tub Henning Christiansen 64-91

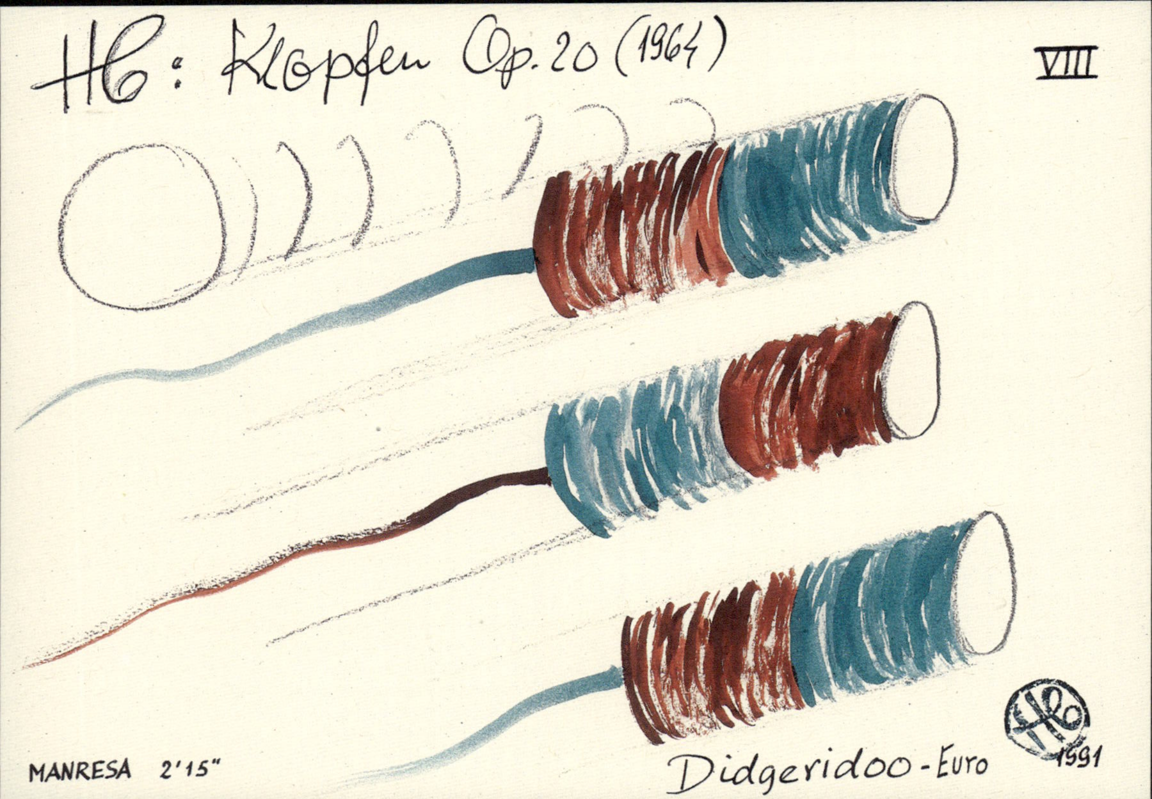

MANRESA 2'15" Digeridoo-Euro HC 1991

This is FLUXUS speaking FLUXUS

Now?
Has Element 2 climbed up to Element 1?
Now?
Has Element 1 climbed down Element 2?

and Element 3

Fat corner / Fat corner
Filter fat corner
Felt corner

Brownspaces

Good morning, where are you going?
: "Thorvaldsen Museum"

I am flying to you too, MANRESA

Hier spricht FLUXUS Fluxus

Nun?
Ist Element 2 zu Element 1 heraufgestiegen?
Nun?
Ist Element 1 zu Element 2 heruntergestiegen?

– und Element 3

Fettecke Fettecke
filterfettecke
filzecke

Braunräume

‚Guden Tag wo gehen Sie hin'?
: "Thorvaldsen Museum"

Auch zu dir fliege ich MANRESA

Henning Christiansen 91 3'32"

[II] + [ ] + IX

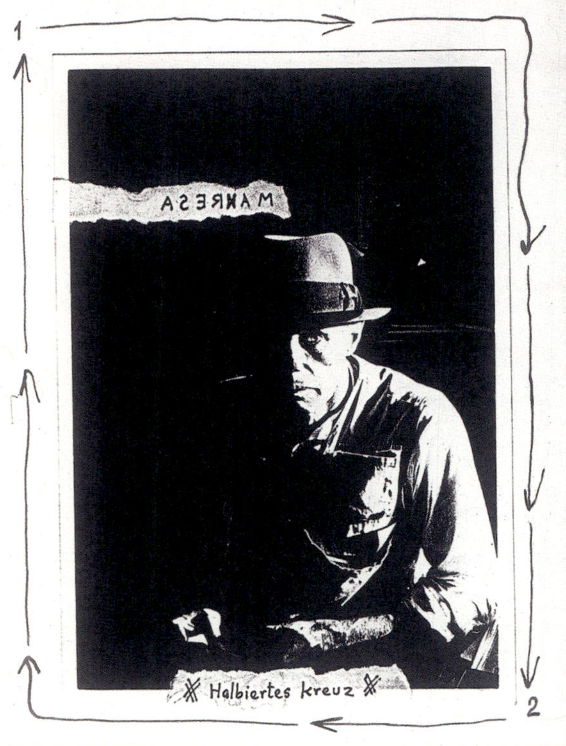

Foto: HC MØN-DK 26.7.82 - Mann auf Reise -

3'32" [II]+[]+IX
Henning Christiansen 91

Halved cross
PHOTO: HC MØN-DK 26/7/82 -Traveling man-

Attain
SILENCE
YOURSELF
and
GO ON -->

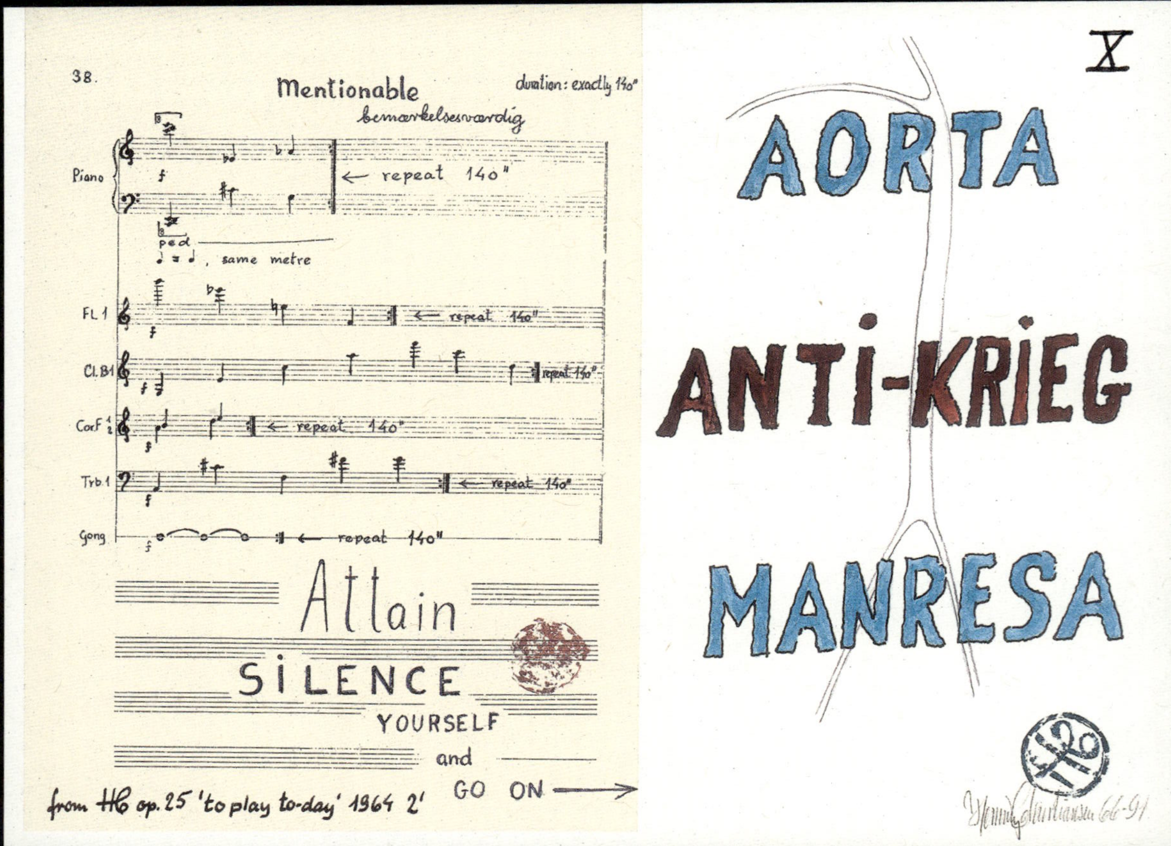

AORTA

ANTI-WAR

MANRESA

from HC op. 25 “to play to-day” 1964 2'

Henning Christiansen 66-91

sic Tone II

Rain music

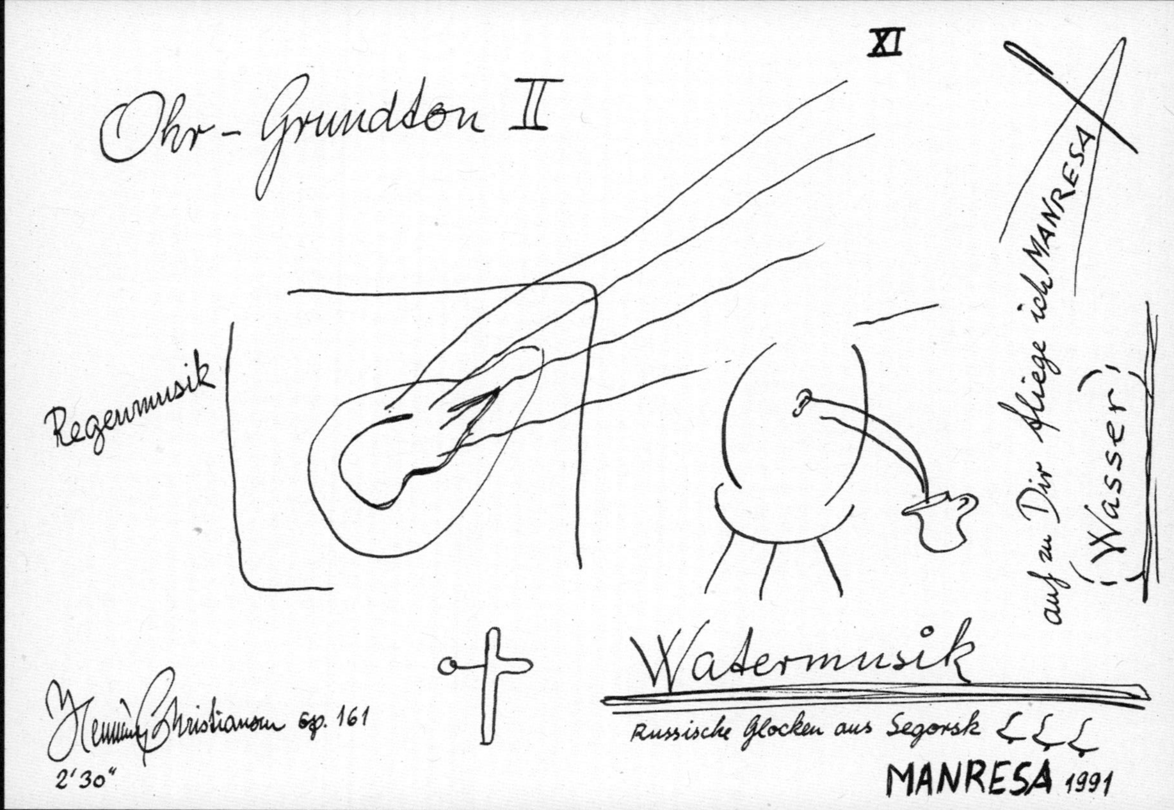

I am flying to you too, MANRESA

Henning Christiansen op. 161
2'30"

Water Music
Russian bells from Zagorsk
MANRESA 1991

MANRESA 1991 [The wounded] Henning Christiansen op. 199
[The traveller]

I	Water Music	0	D: 20
	green ear vase		
	Ear - BASIC TONE I (HC op. 161)	1’2”	1’35”
II	This is FLUXUS speaking (Indian Rattle)	1’27”	D: 20
	MANRESA (J.B.)	4’57”	3’32”
III	Suitcase with a halved cross [The traveller]	4’58”	D: 03
	(Indian Rattle) [The wounded]		
	Space and Object (HC von op. 28)	9’33”	4’35”
IV	Counting-Song (Birds singing)	9’30”	D: 03
	for 3 voices + tape		
	Dialectical Evolution Ib (HC op. 16)	13’23”	3’50”
V	Reading of the text ‘Time’	13’20”	D: 34
	Next Point (HC op. 28)	17’20”	4’
VI	Choir - plaster feet walk	17’15”	D: 03
	for 2 voices + tape		
	I can’t (HJN) Steps (BN) Stone Age Gramophone (HC)	18’40”	1’30”
VII	8 air pumps × 2 (fat)	18’35”	D: 03
	On the Line (HC von op. 28)	22’35”	4’
VIII	DIGERIDOO	22’30”	D: 45
	Beats (HC op. 20) 1964	23’30”	2’15”
IX	This is FLUXUS speaking (Beats, Indian Rattle)	23’45”	D: 70
	MANRESA (J.B.)	27’16”	3’32”
X	AORTA ANTI-WAR MANRESA	27’17”	D: 03
	PIPE CALL		
	Mentionable (HC von op. 25)	28’	2’
XI	Water Music (Russian bells, Zagorsk)	28’	D: 20
	green ear vase	fade up - down	
	Ear - BASIC TONE II (HC op. 161)	~30’	2’30”

bird screeching

FIRST STATION:
SHRINE NOSTRA SENYORA DE LA GUIA

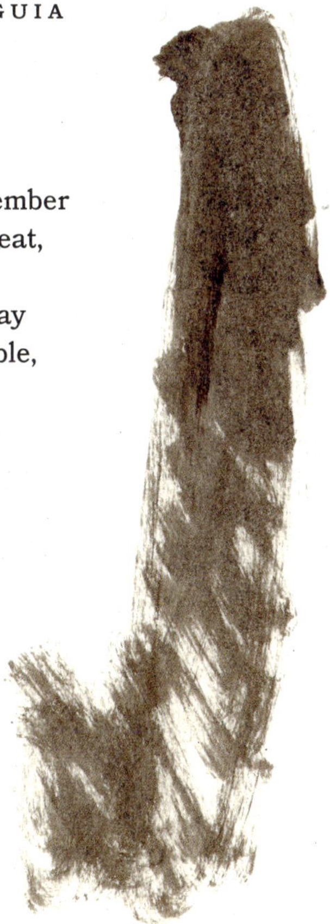

A little Church – Chapel
Before the altar a table — altar = table — to remember the altar as a table. All of us, every day, when we eat, when we work at our tables alone or together, we are also all sitting at the altar in a spiritual way
→ so the table is the dining table, the working table, the altar, the last supper.

The empty table ←→ altar
The social — the common elements
The beginning, the empty table

•

Plaster on the table
The creation
— water + mineral (earth) plaster without any different form is worked out with the hands on the table
— Process + material → ? → Object? Form? Structure? Experience? Exercise? (Element 3?)

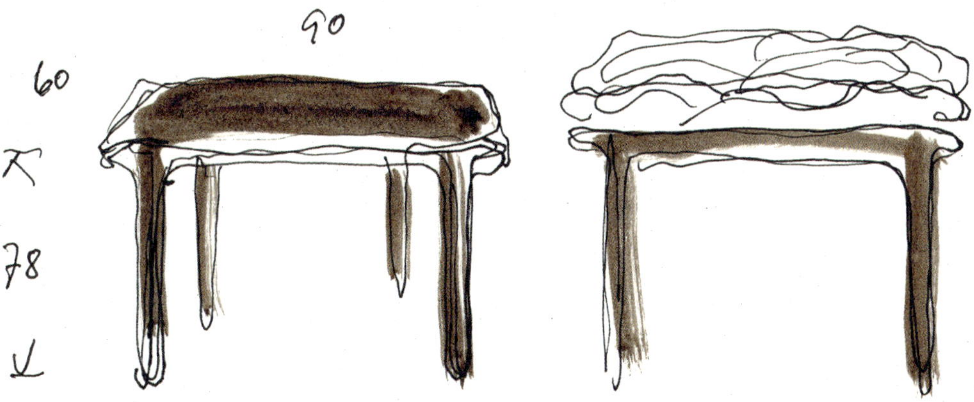

•

Seven red roses → the Crown of Thorns → the rose action by Beuys → for your lover → ...
The Jewish element in our spiritual tradition → ...

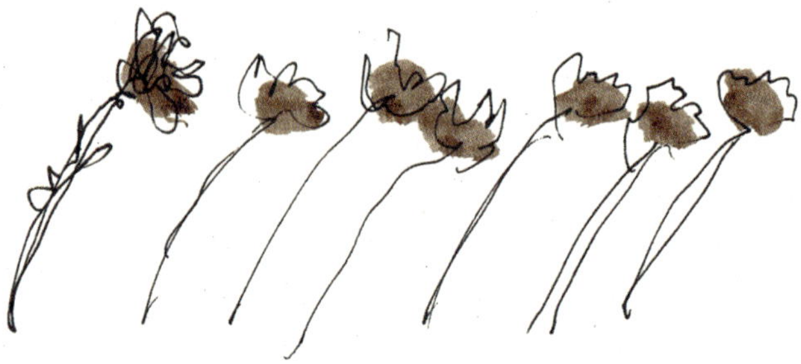

•

The roses will be placed in the middle of the table in the plaster before it hardens completely.

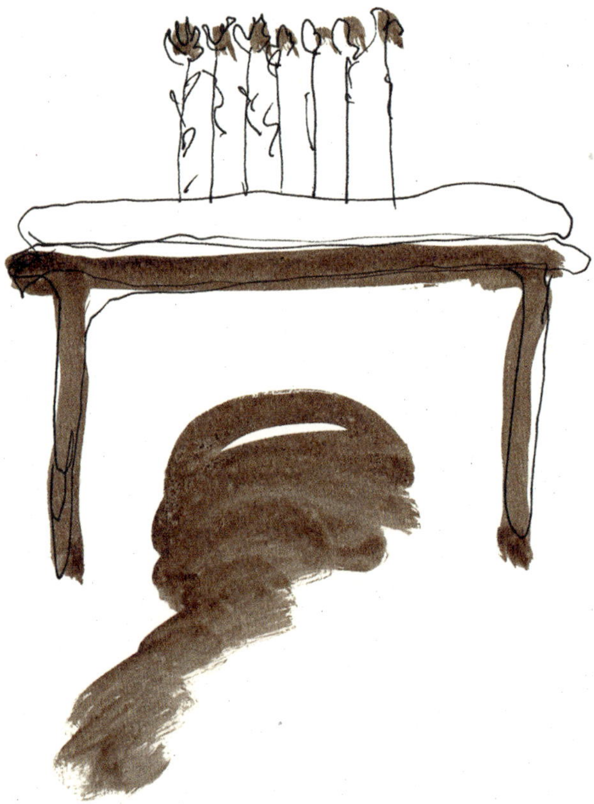

●

Twelve white cups will be placed on the table — water will be poured in the cups — I will cut my left thumb and drip a drop of blood in every cup.

the last supper → the altar
→ the object ←→ the persons

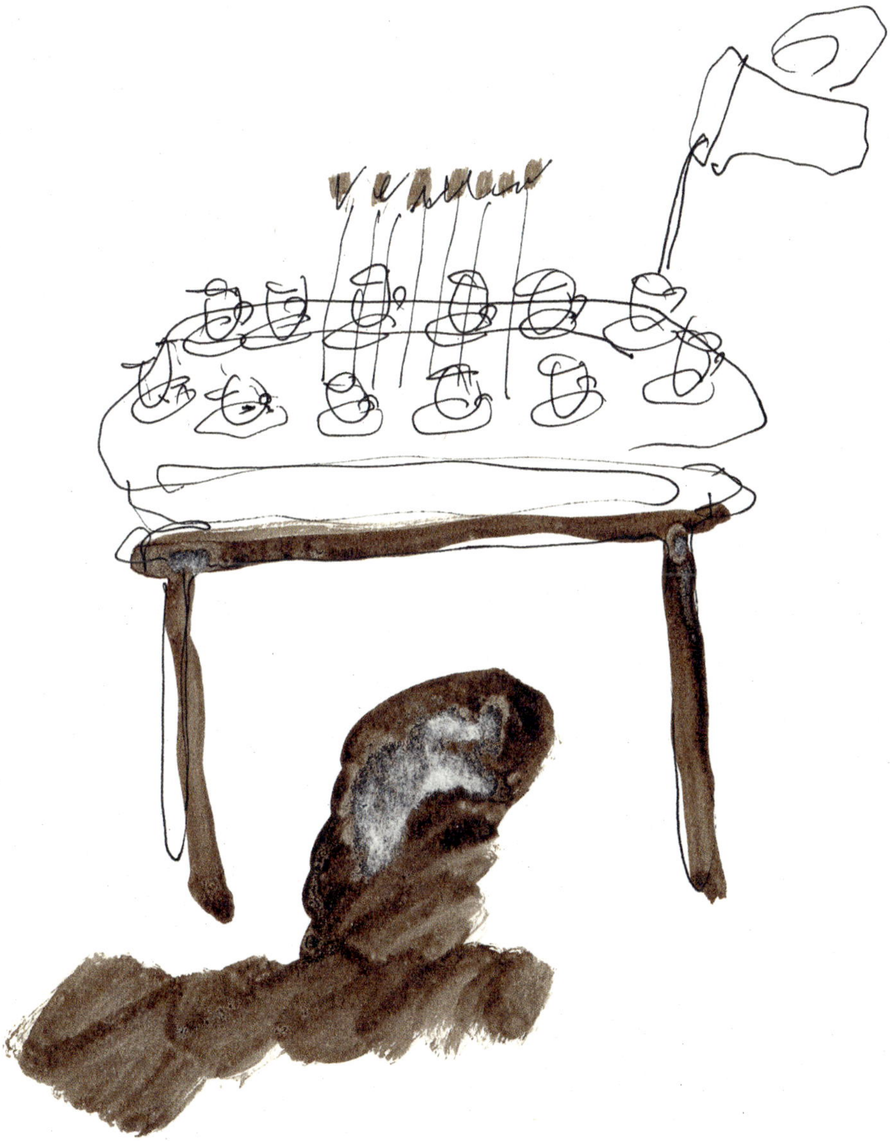

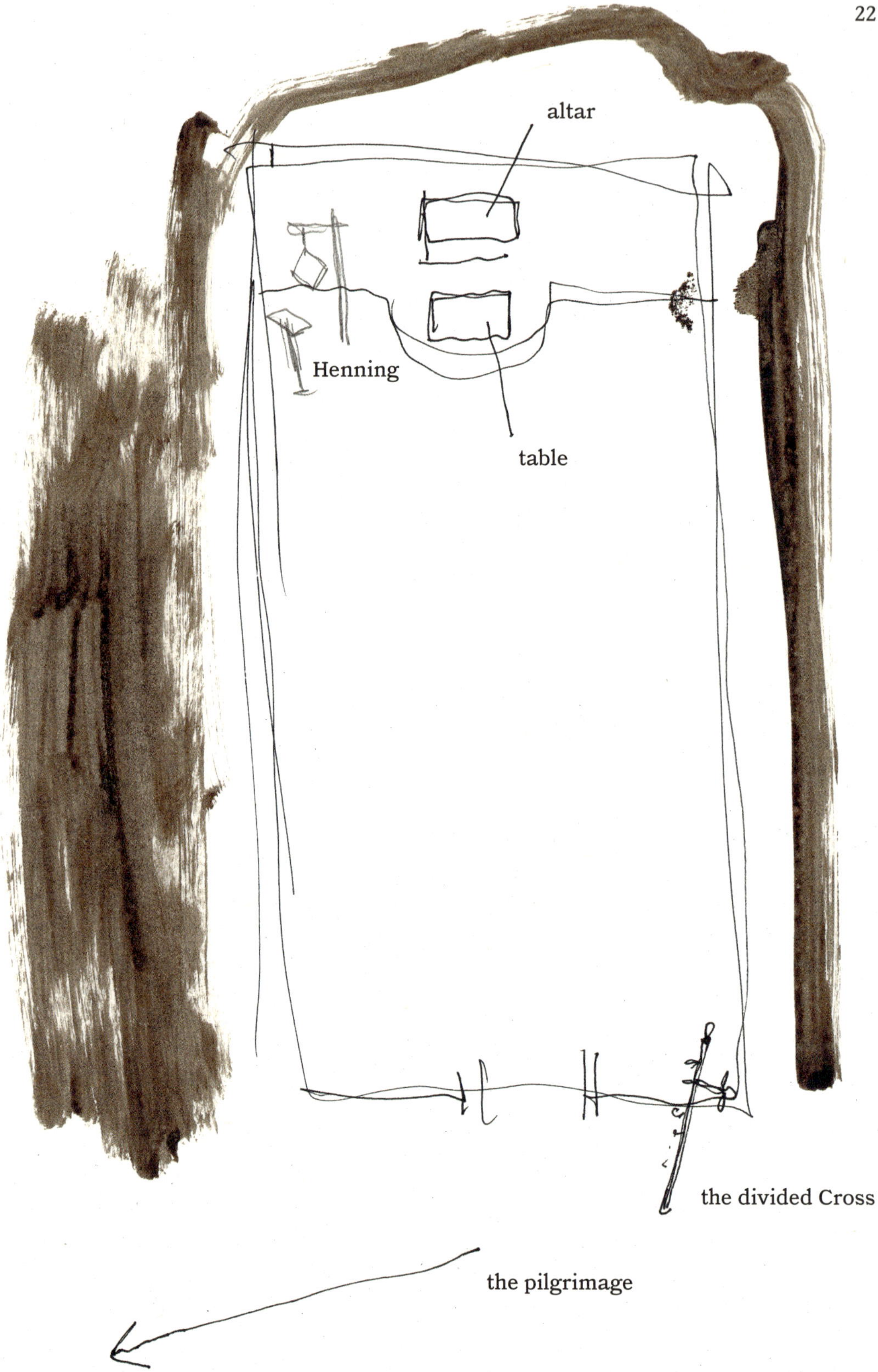

Henning and I are dragging the cross to River Cardener.
(Six more people are needed because of the weight, 240 kg)

SECOND STATION: RIVER CARDENER

Arriving with the cross.
First we will put fire to the boat.

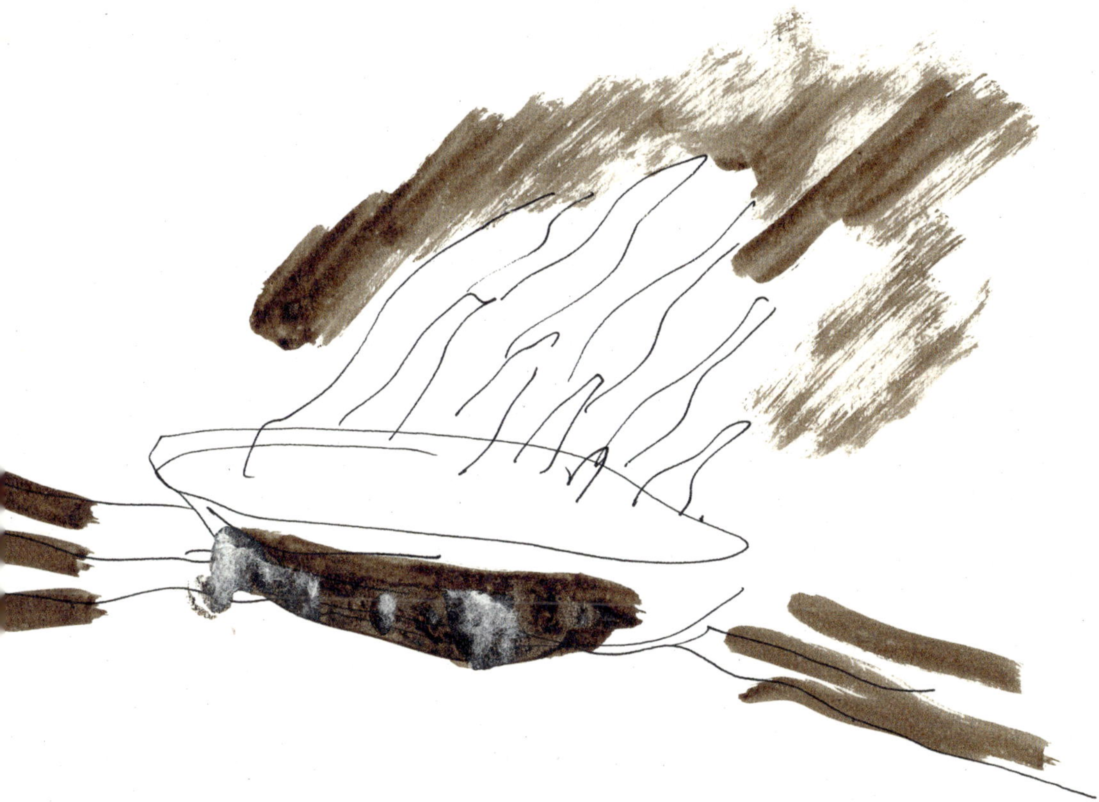

●

Literally the enlightenment of the Cardener
but also the purification through fire of the boat that
we are arriving in from the North
it was here earlier as a way to bury people (of course
those days nobleman, and so on...).

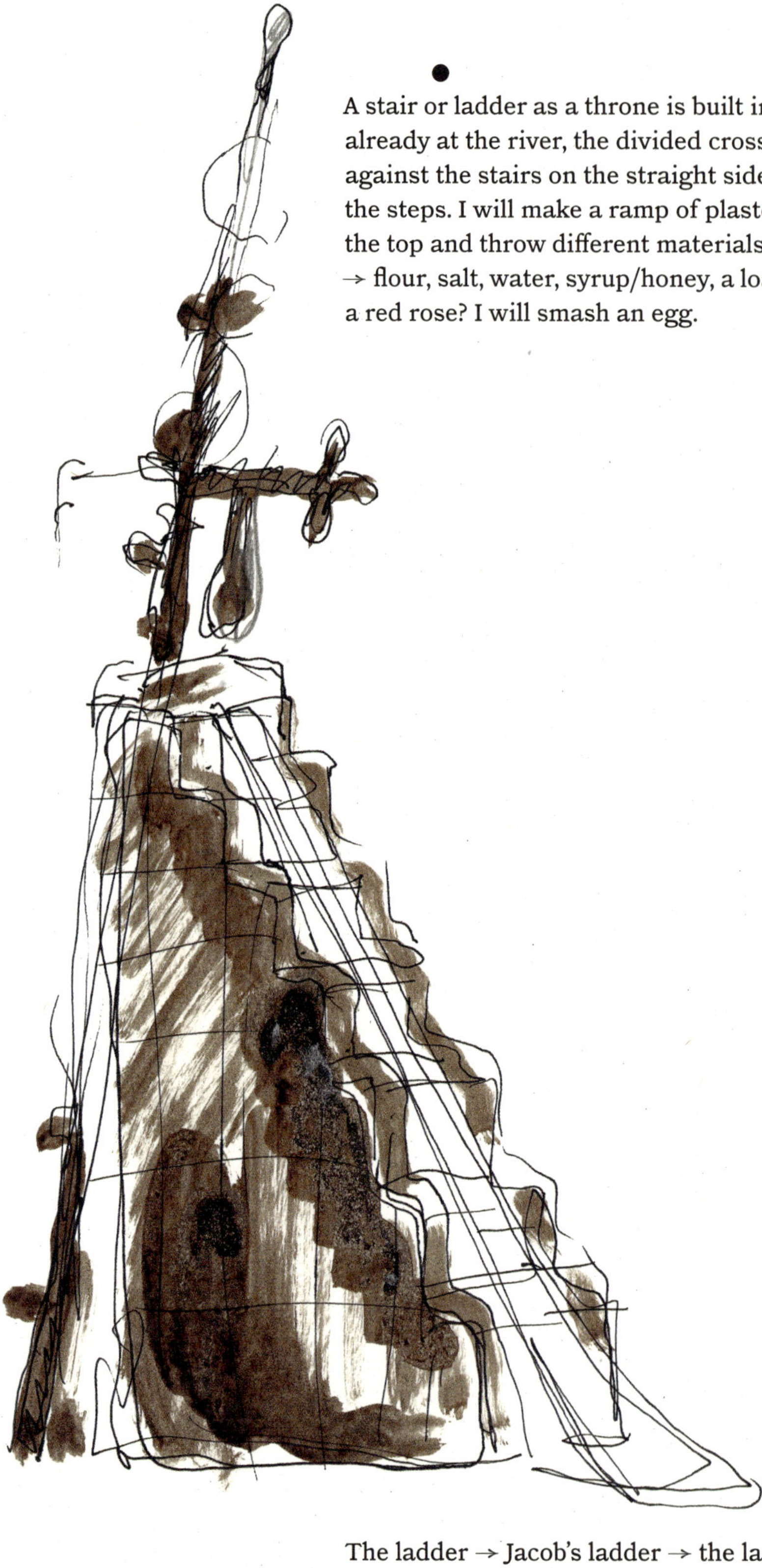

A stair or ladder as a throne is built in stone and is already at the river, the divided cross will be raised against the stairs on the straight side, on the side with the steps. I will make a ramp of plaster, I will crawl to the top and throw different materials down this ramp → flour, salt, water, syrup/honey, a loaf of bread, a fish, a red rose? I will smash an egg.

The ladder → Jacob's ladder → the ladder to heaven → our aim for a higher spiritual experience → the enlightenment of the Cardener → but also the pulpit → the Sermon on the Mount

Twelve pieces of sackcloth will one by one be dipped in the river and one by one thrown against the cliffs → John the Baptist → to baptise → to join the community (the spiritual) → to go out and make all the people ... → On each piece of sackcloth will be thrown salt, a loaf of bread, 2 fish and a cross of plaster will be made ... To find a group, a community, with a spiritual and practical vision → the Society of Jesus

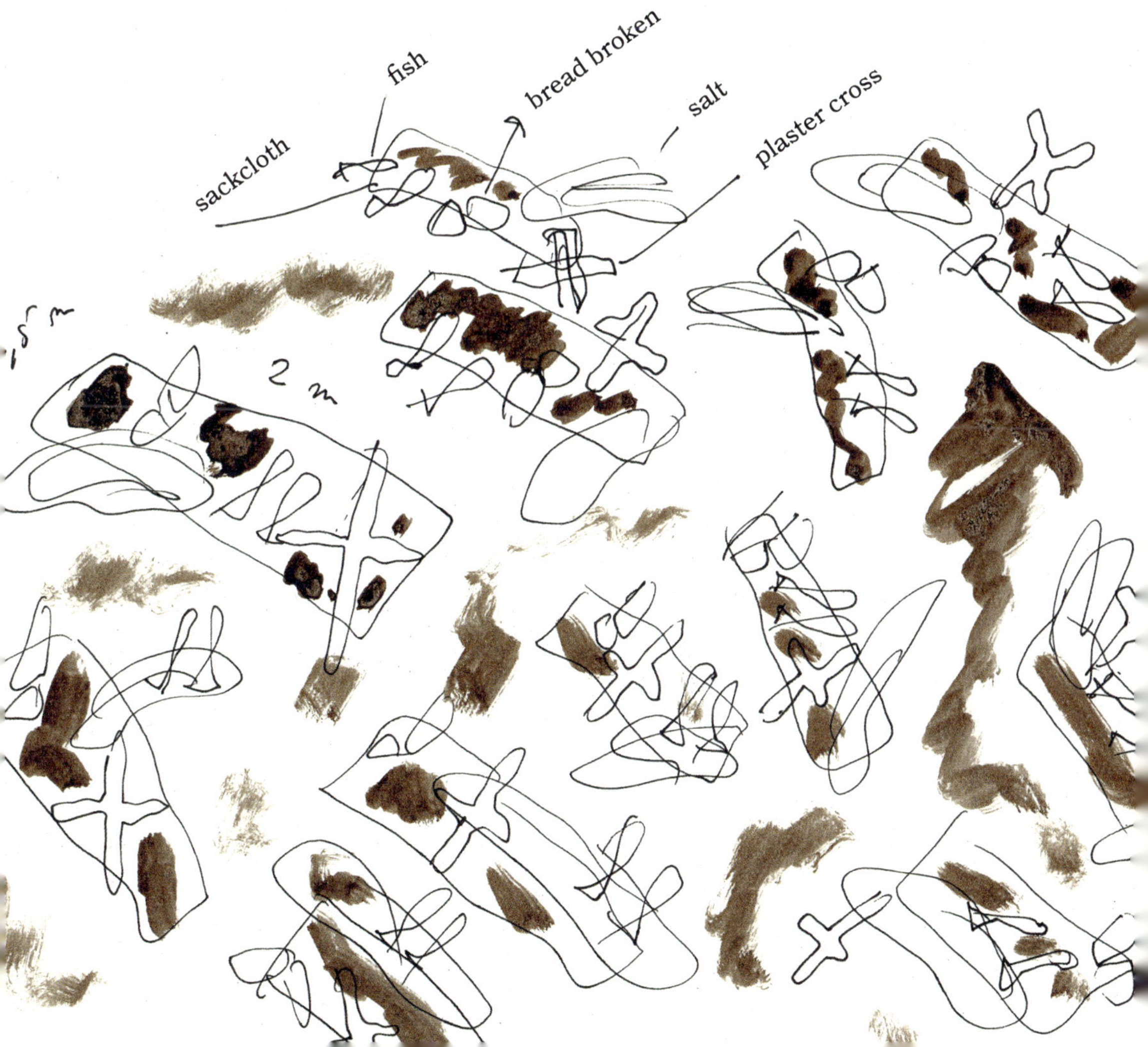

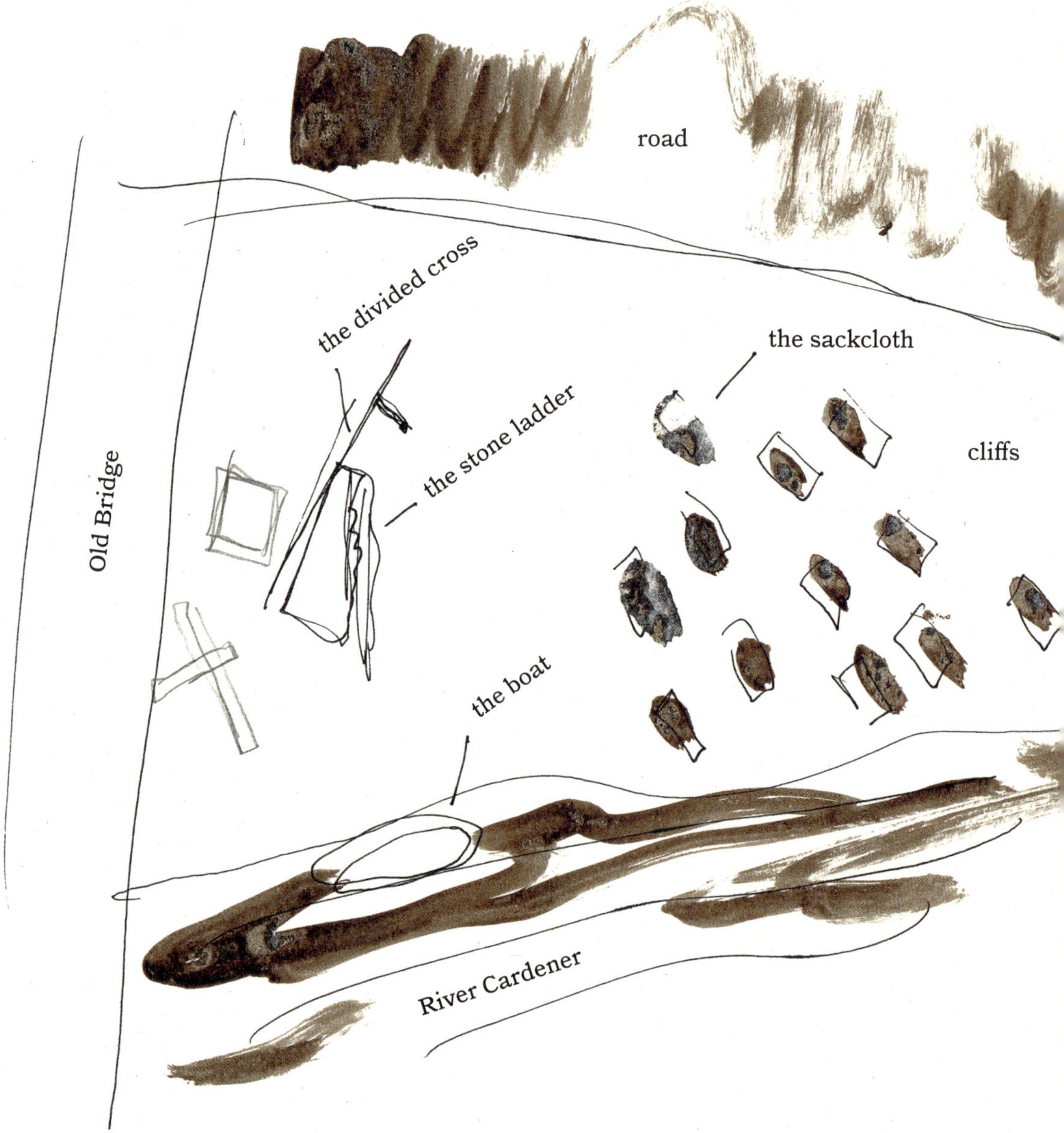
road
the divided cross
the sackcloth
the stone ladder
cliffs
Old Bridge
the boat
River Cardener

THIRD STATION: OLD BRIDGE

I take a white dove from its cage and let it go →
give it its freedom → to liberate the spirit

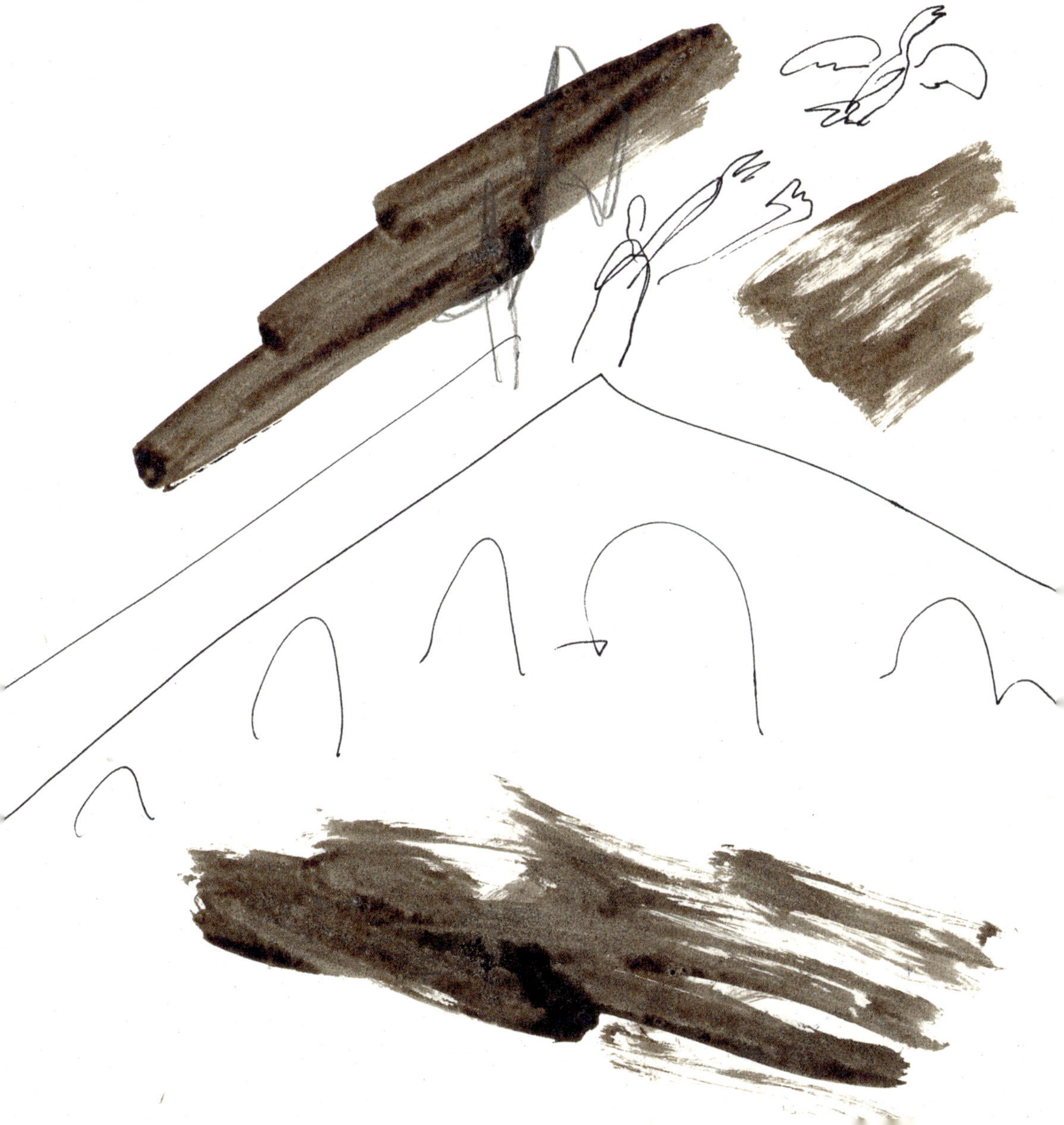

FOURTH STATION:
HOLY CAVE

My part of the original MANRESA from 1966, *Sculptural Demonstration no. 1*, carried out first at Copenhagen St. Kongensgade 101, in an arrangement called Tilstande where more artists participated ... Henning and also Beuys who one day did his *Siberian Symphonie*. After that he invited Henning and me to MANRESA in Düsseldorf, I think it was because my Sculptural Demonstrations with my feet were an example how an artist through 'artistic' or 'spiritual' exercises can work with art in a new way and that was an important part of the European Fluxus ...

Different materials will be worked on with the feet.

●

I walk the line on bottles.

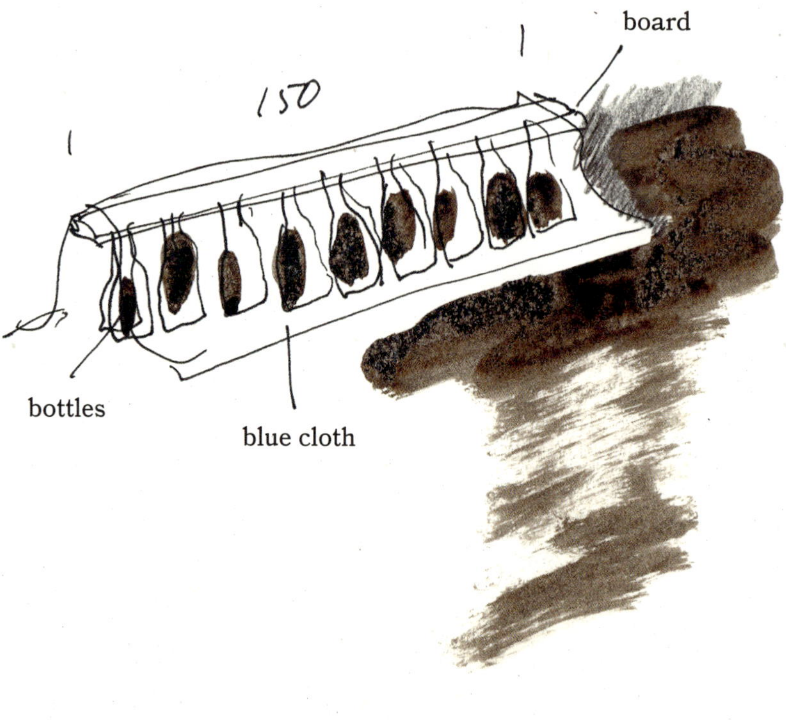

•

I smash electric bulbs with my feet.

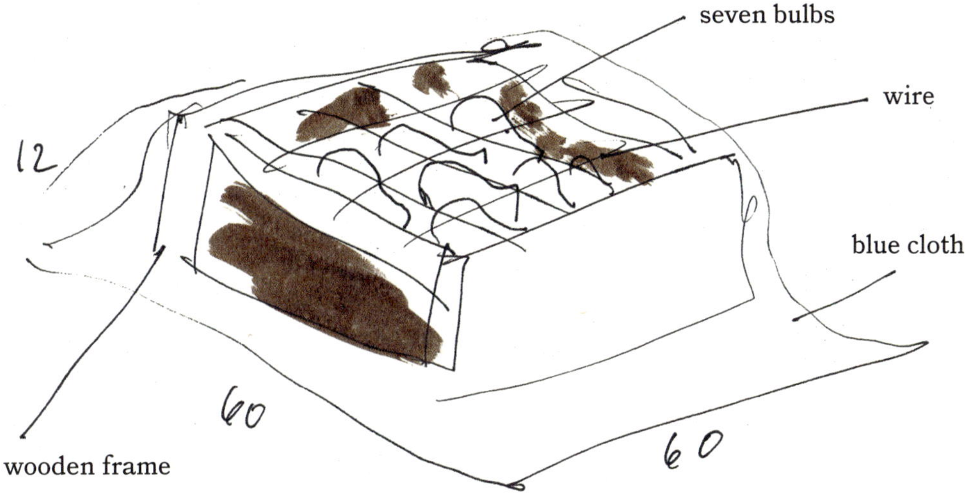

•

I am stamping on a cube of clay covered by blue cloth.

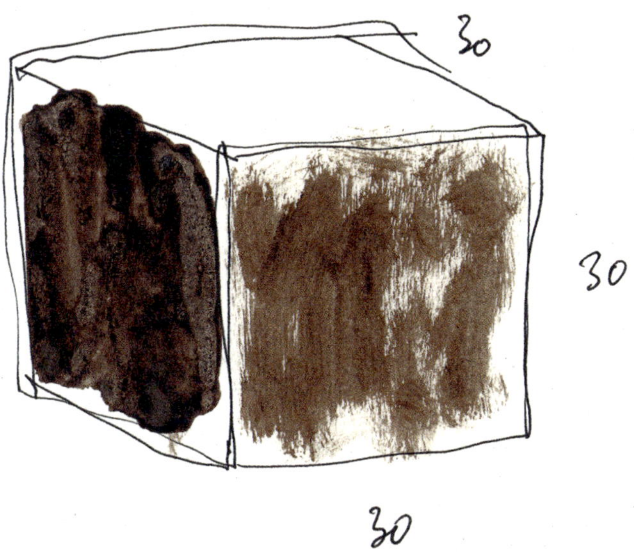

•

I am stamping in flour.

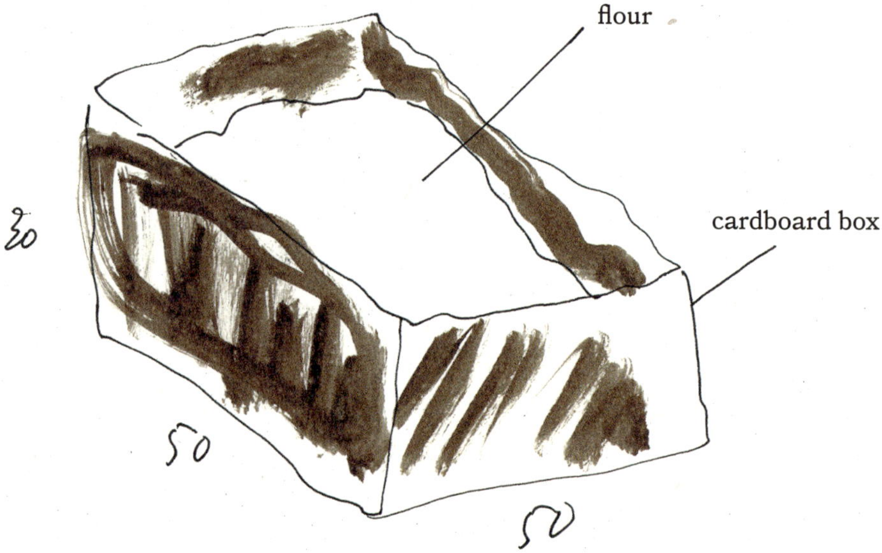

•

I will smear crystal soap over a Masonite plate with the felt.

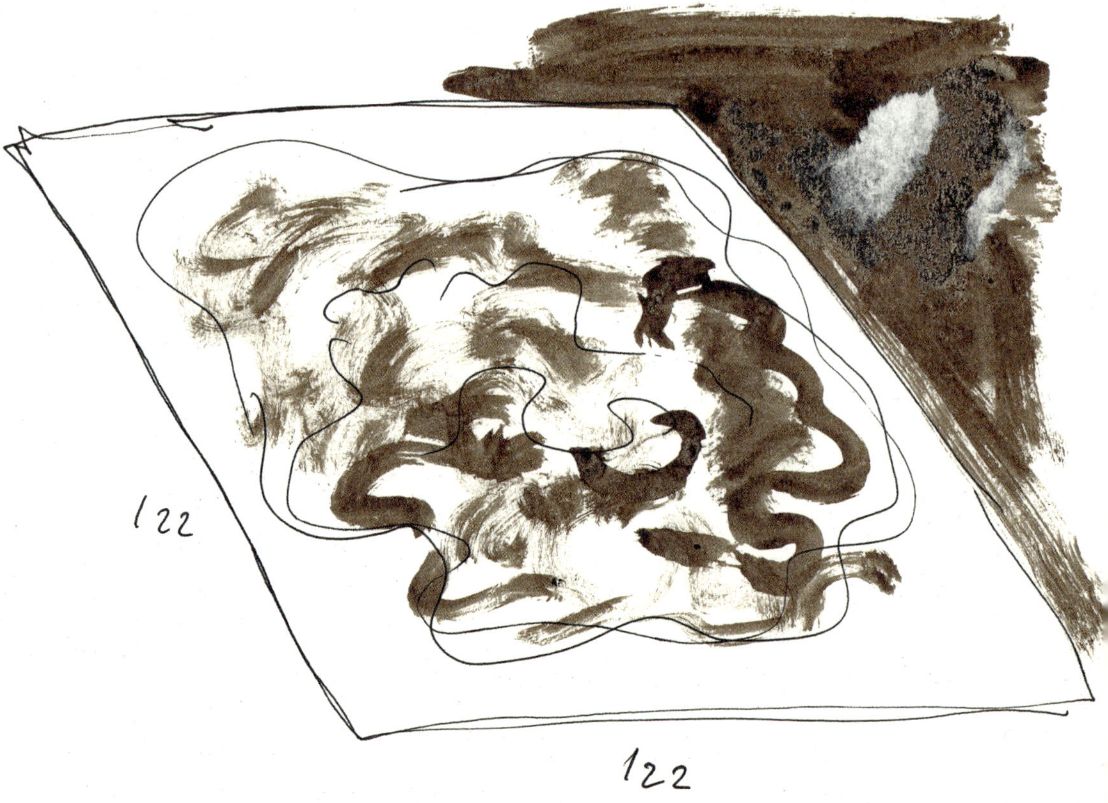

• I will splash the water with my feet.

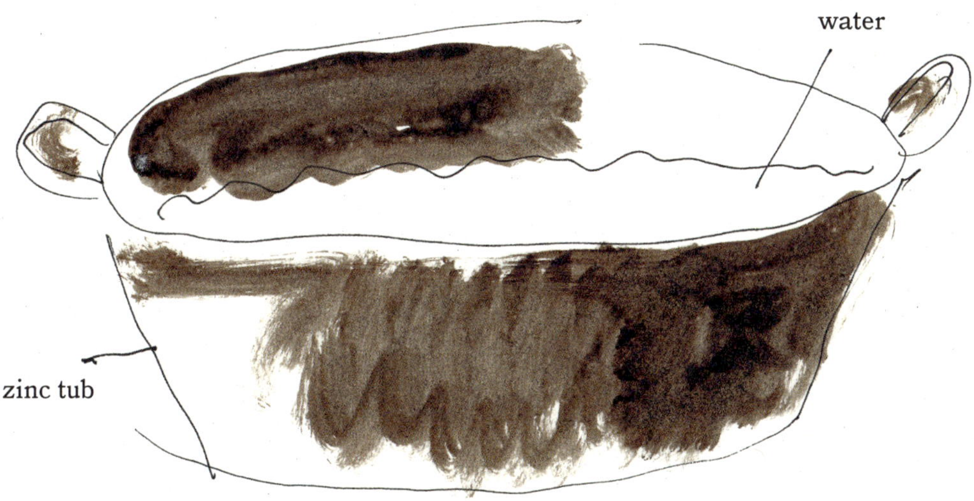

• I will cast my feet into two plaster blocks.

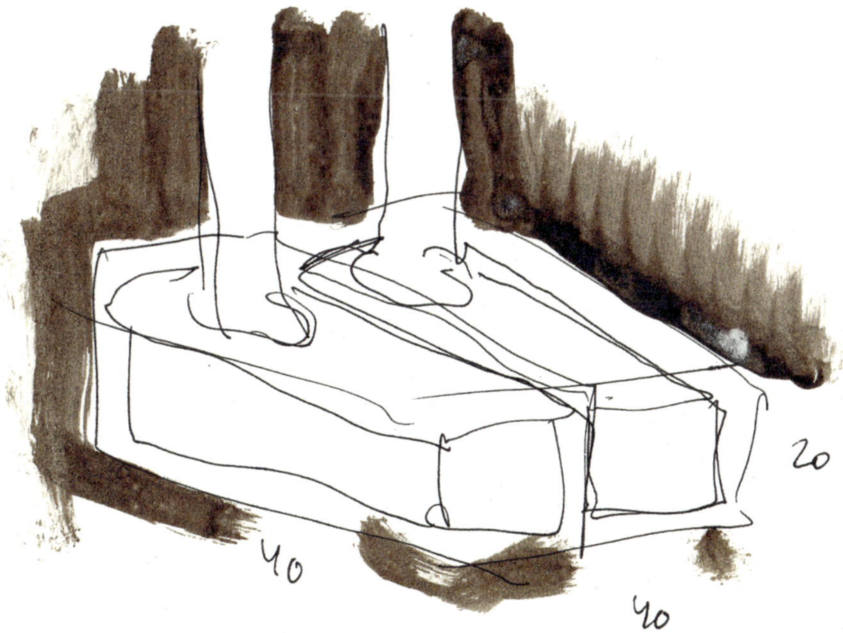

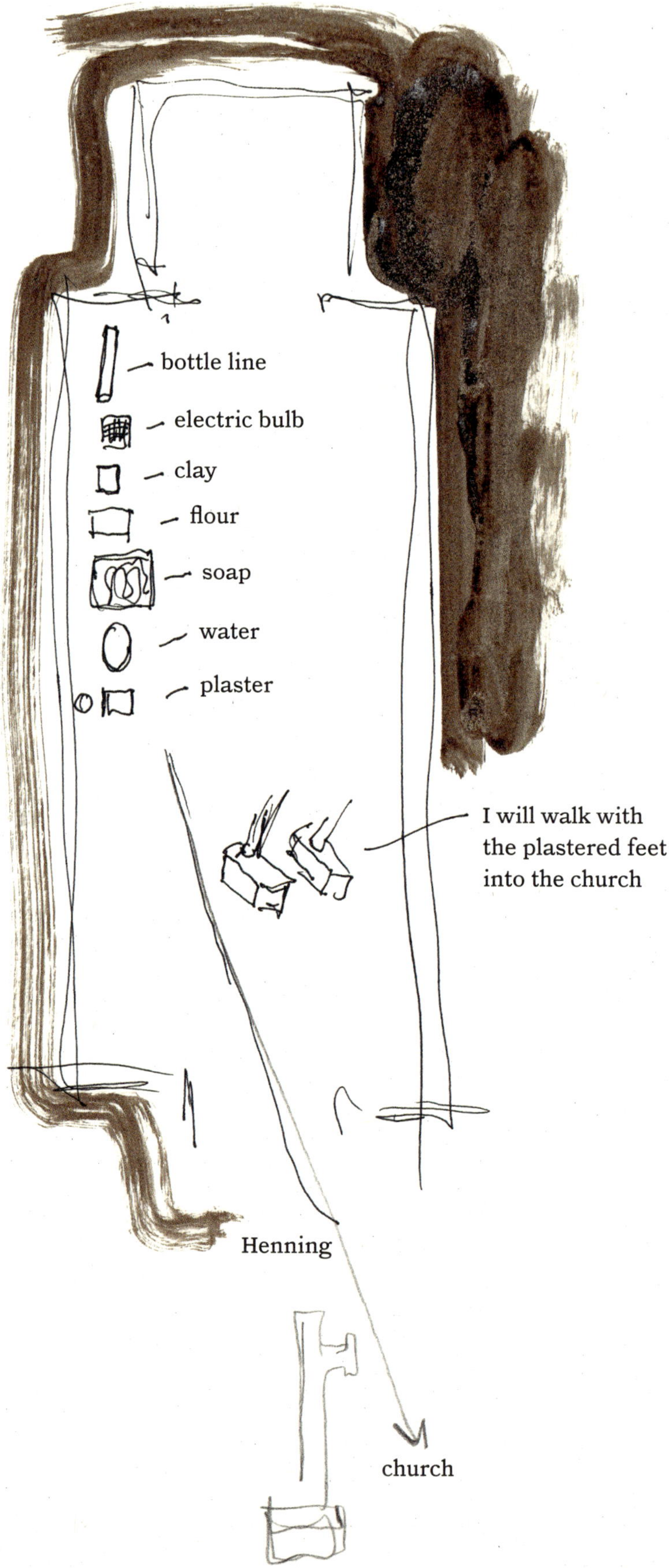
bottle line
electric bulb
clay
flour
soap
water
plaster
I will walk with
the plastered feet
into the church
Henning
church

FIFTH STATION: THE CHURCH

Before the altar I will build a bed of clay and place three mirrors on it. Then I will make a long line of plaster with a spiral on the end, on the line I will make some elements in plaster, a house, a ramp, three tops, two cupolas, one triangle. I will make twelve heaps of gravel, place a pane of glass in each of them, and over each pane crack an egg. I will smash the three mirrors on the clay bed, pour syrup over the broken pieces. Then I put plaster and sackcloth around one leg (the right), my stomach and over my left shoulder and then I will lay down on the clay bed with the syrup and broken pieces of glass.

This action is developed during a series of actions Henning and I did together called *Tiefland*, a kind of homage to Beuys, that he and Henning should have done before his death — so this bed is maybe the death of Beuys but also when he was wounded and then also when Ignatius was wounded, but it is also sleep, and the dream, the visions that appear in us or maybe [are] sent to us — ... the dream and meditation → but also Jesus in the boat on Lake Kinneret sleeping while the storm is hard there, in many interpretations.

The plaster line, *Eurasienstab*, the life line, a symbol on the way we all must walk — Ignatius walking from Montserrat to Manresa?

The twelve heaps of gravel with a pane of glass and eggs → from dust to dust, from earth to earth → the glass as the invisible soul, the egg the creation and the destruction.

There are many possible ways to read those elements in this creation — which in a way started in 1966.

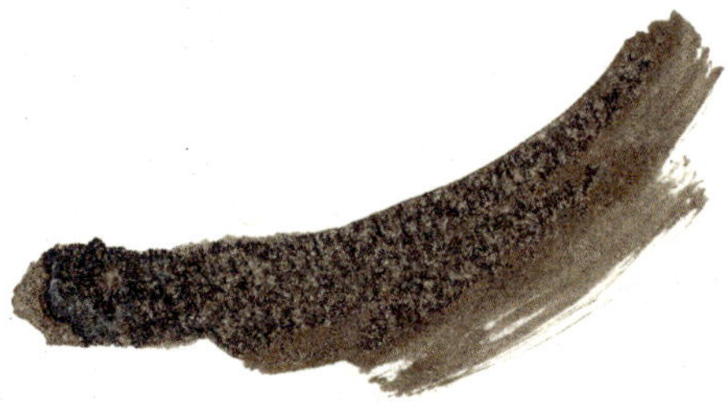

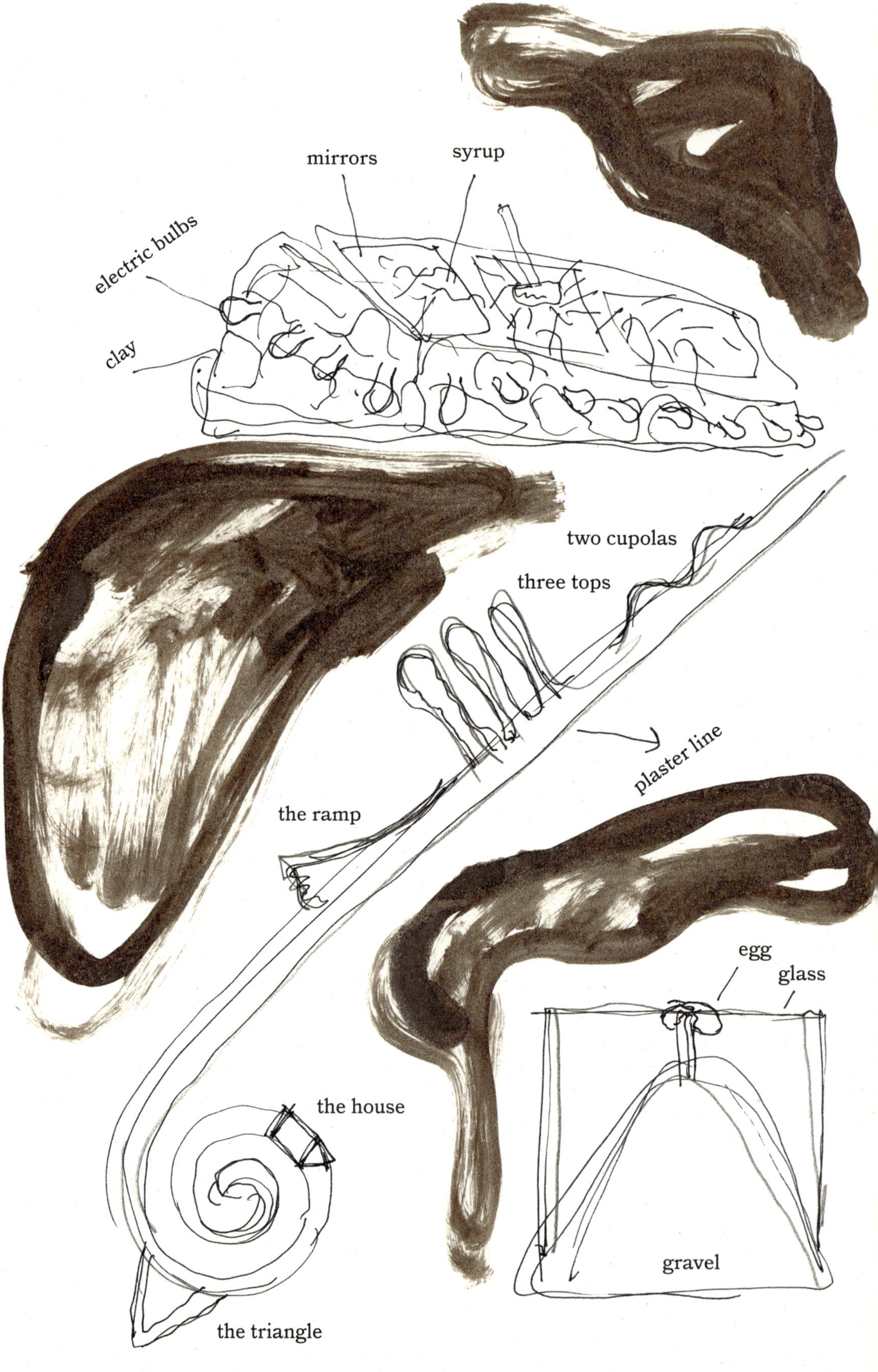
mirrors
syrup
electric bulbs
clay
two cupolas
three tops
plaster line
the ramp
egg
glass
the house
gravel
the triangle

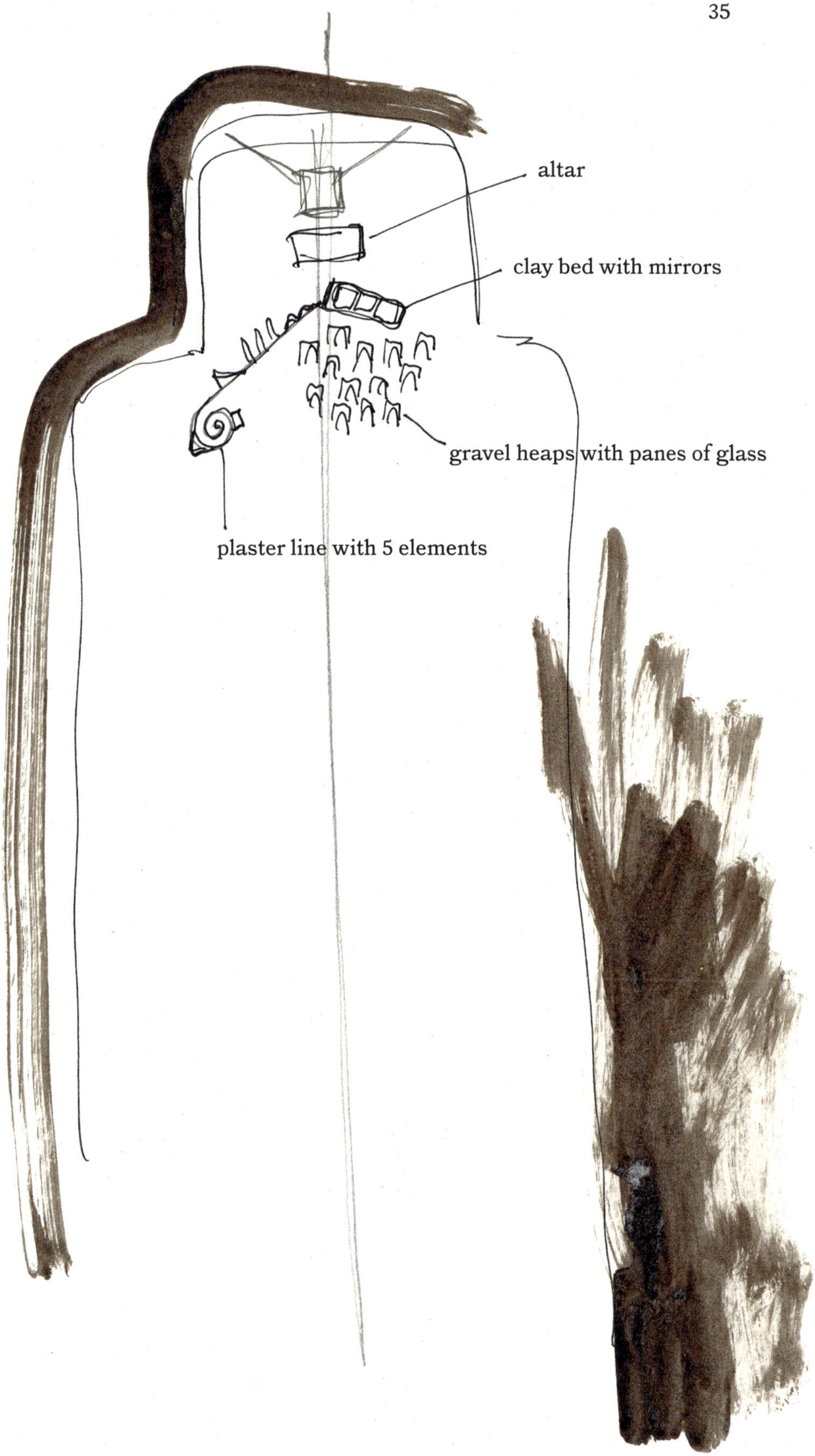
altar
clay bed with mirrors
gravel heaps with panes of glass
plaster line with 5 elements

SIXTH STATION:
THE FIREPLACE

bread and fish → the Sermon on the Mount →

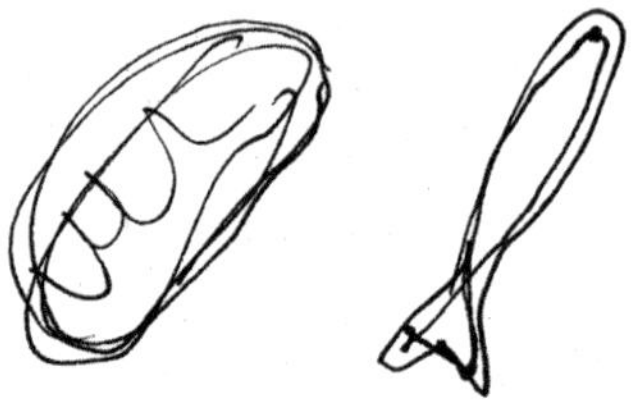

... that which you can not talk about — about that
you must remain silent ...

(almost from L. W.)

Sculptural Demonstrations ←→ Spiritual Exercises

Bjørn Nørgaard, illustrated preparatory
script for the action *Manresa Hbf*, 1994.

MANRESA
4. 11. 94

(1) GUIA-church

a table ca. 60×90 cm high ca. 78 cm (solid wood)
1 sack of plaster of paris (modellplaster) escayola.
12 white coffee-cups + (undercups) –
1 Glas-can (ca. 2 Liter) ferro d'ai fre
7 red roses
salledo · 1 buckett (ca. 12 Liters) (1 whipstick) batidora (Water)
1 metallplate 40×40 cm with a cornerhole
thick 3 mm
stativ - Foto a "chair"

(2) Rio Cardener – on the clif.

from Denmark, made in Denmark:
cast iron-cross (5 m)
yellow cross (wooden) called: Yellow point
1 Teddybear
in MANRESA:
1 metallplate 1 m² thick 1,5 mm iron – iron oxide
a big stone (100 × 40 × 25 cm ca. – picapedrer
1 liter yellow paint (yellow ochre-chalk-paint) ocre
27 stone (ca. 20×20×80 cm)
Sisó como:

15 sacks of plaster of paris (modellplaster) 25 kg.
3 bucketts (ca. 12 Liters) salledes.
Sack-clothes (jute) (ruf strucktur) –
12 pieces each ca. 2 m × 1,5 m
1 m³ salt
24 fish *
12 bred 1 kg. rodó
Wood for fire or an old boat (will be burned)

(3) Pont Vell

1 metallplate 70×70 (½ mm thick) cornerhole
1 White dove in a cage
1 white flag (made in Denmark)

(4) Santa Cova

12 beerbotles (Estrella. Buides).
2 laths (2 m long 2 × 12 cm) ↳ llistó (fusta).
1 roll Steelwire 0,5 mm ↳ rotllo filferro
1 masoniteplate 122×122 cm
7 kg Christall soap →
5 kg flour → farina
1 big metall – with water – zinc (gibrell).

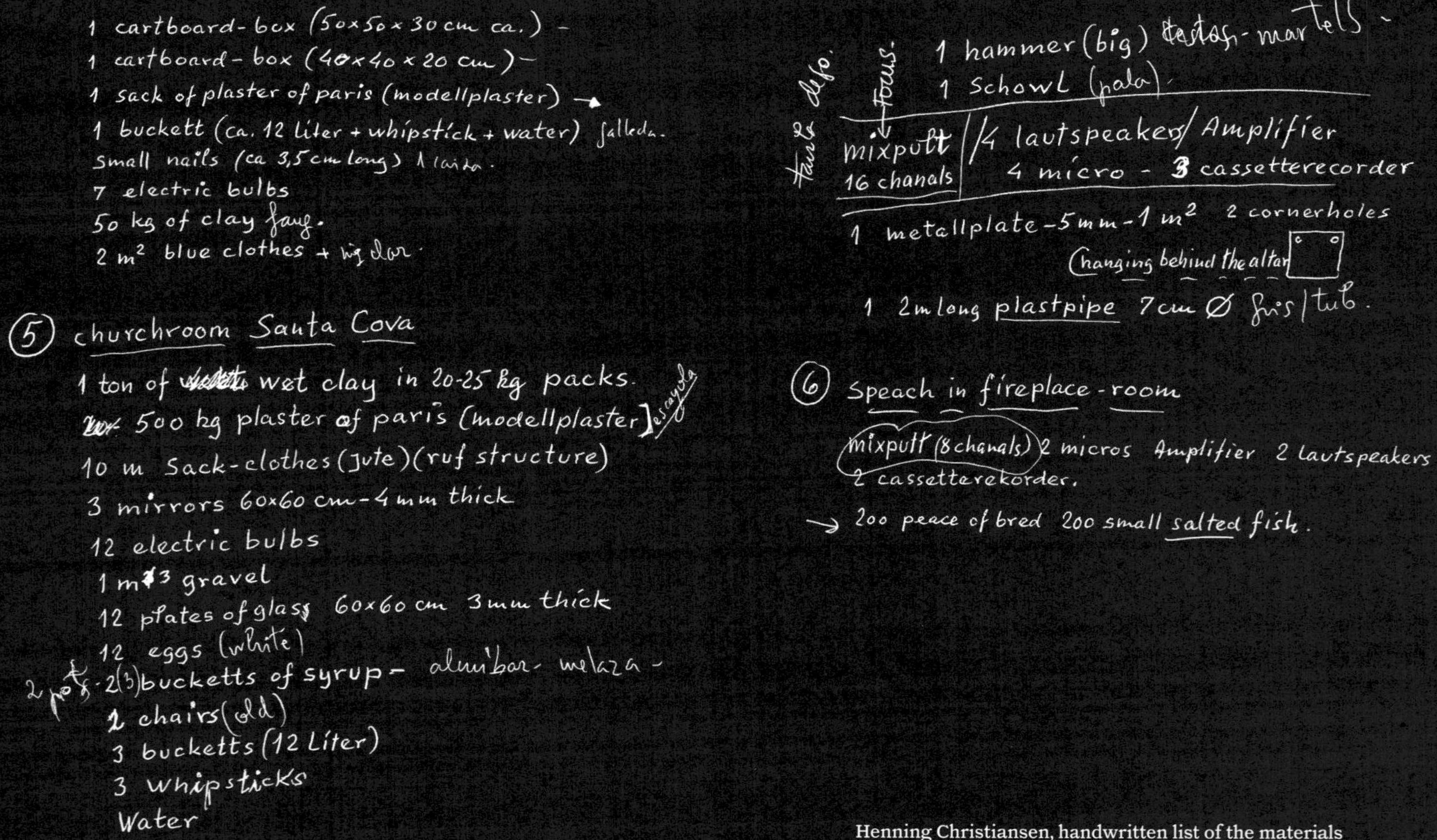

1 cartboard-box (50×50×30 cm ca.) -
1 cartboard-box (40×40×20 cm)-
1 sack of plaster of paris (modellplaster) →
1 buckett (ca. 12 liter + whipstick + water) galleda.
small nails (ca 3,5 cm long) 1 caixa.
7 electric bulbs
50 kg of clay fang.
2 m² blue clothes + higdor.

(5) churchroom Santa Cova

1 ton of wet clay in 20-25 kg packs.
500 kg plaster of paris (modellplaster] escayola
10 m Sack-clothes (jute)(ruf structure)
3 mirrors 60×60 cm - 4 mm thick
12 electric bulbs
1 m³ gravel
12 plates of glass 60×60 cm 3 mm thick
12 eggs (white)
2 pots · 2(3) bucketts of syrup - almíbar - melaza -
2 chairs (old)
3 bucketts (12 Liter)
3 whipsticks
Water

tank 2 dep. / focus

1 hammer (big) testos - martells -
1 Schowl (pala).

mixpult 16 chanals | 4 lautspeaker / Amplifier
4 micro - 3 cassetterecorder

1 metallplate - 5 mm - 1 m² 2 cornerholes
(hanging behind the altar)

1 2 m long plastpipe 7 cm Ø fris/tub.

(6) Speach in fireplace-room

mixpult (8 chanals) 2 micros Amplifier 2 lautspeakers
2 cassetterekorder.

→ 200 peace of bred 200 small salted fish.

Henning Christiansen, handwritten list of the materials required for the action *Manresa Hbf*, 1994.

HENNING CHRISTIANSEN AND BJØRN NØRGAARD

MANRESA HBF (HOMAGE TO JOSEPH BEUYS AND IGNATIUS OF LOYOLA)

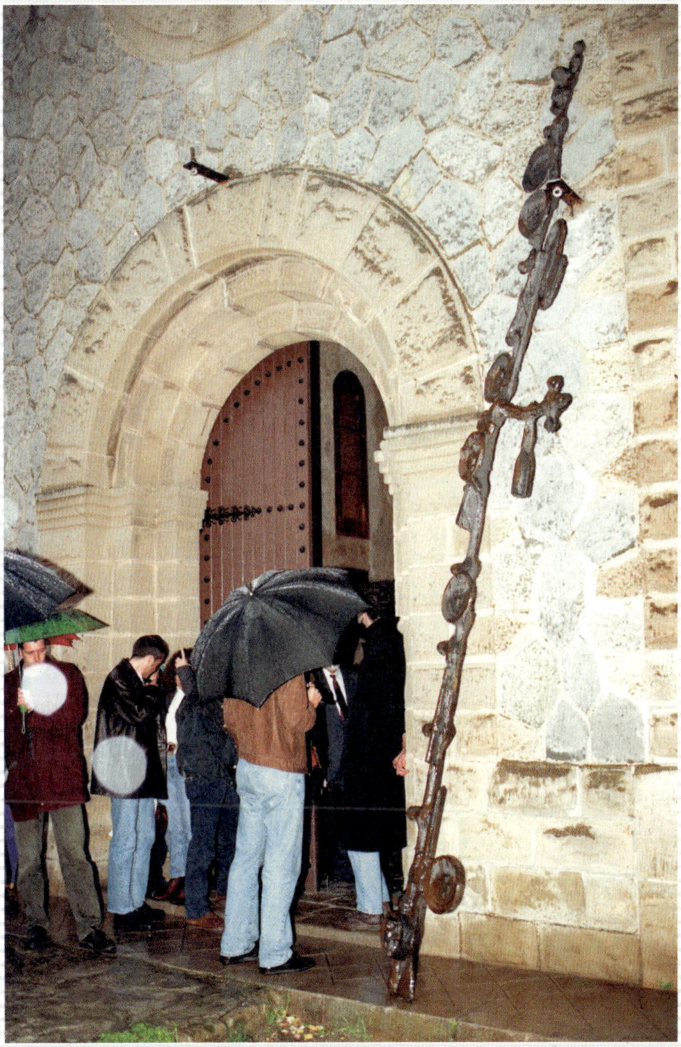

MANRESA iron cross leaning against the church.
H.C. and B.N. drag it to River Cardener on the road.

Manresa, 4 November 1994.

(Photo captions from the handwritten notes by Henning Christiansen)

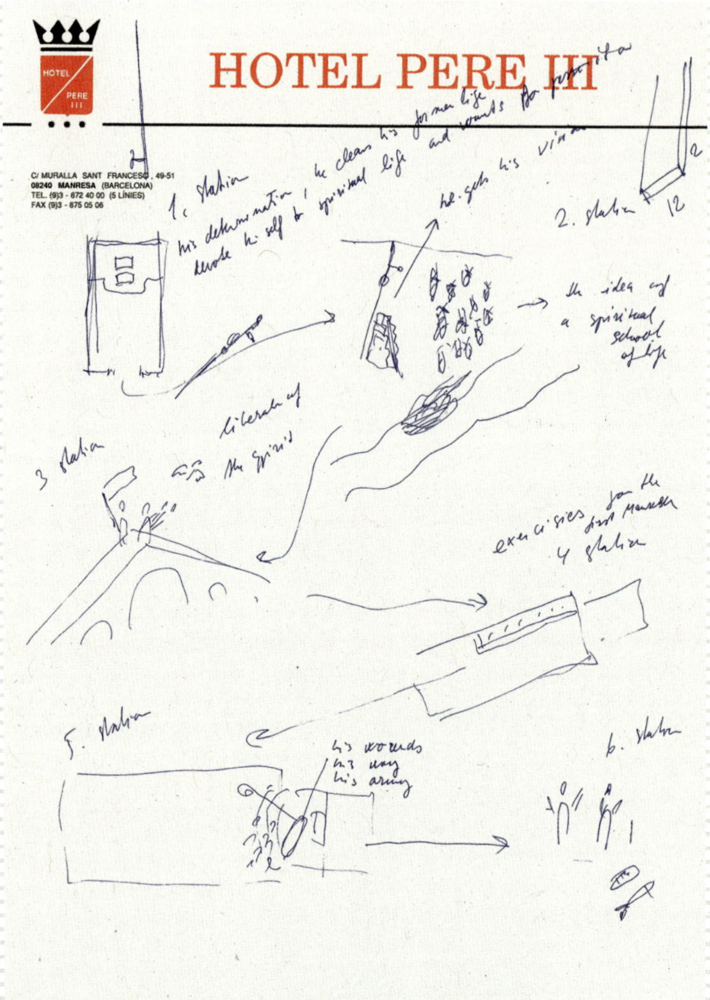

Bjørn Nørgaard, scheme for the 5 stations, created at Manresa a few days before the action.

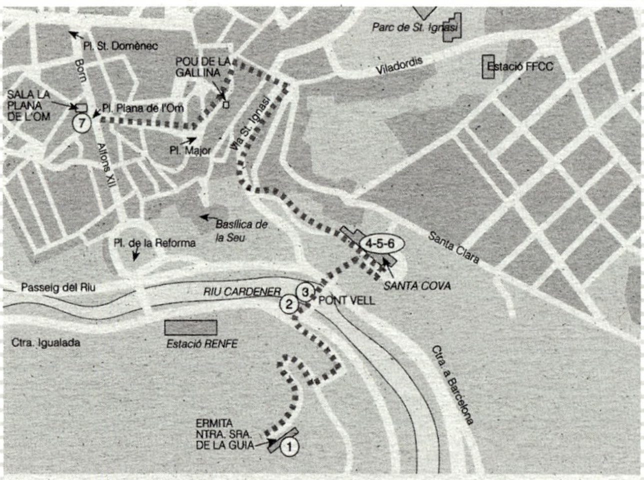

RECORREGUT DE L'ACCIÓ MANRESA

❶ Ermita Ntra. Sra. de la Guia ❷ Pont Vell. Balmes del riu Cardener ❸ Pont Vell ❹ Santa Cova ❺ Església de la Cova ❻ Sala de la llar de foc de la Casa d'Exercicis ❼ Sala "La Plana de l'Om". Plaça Plana de l'Om, 5. Manresa

Map with the different stations of the performance, included in the invitation to the event.

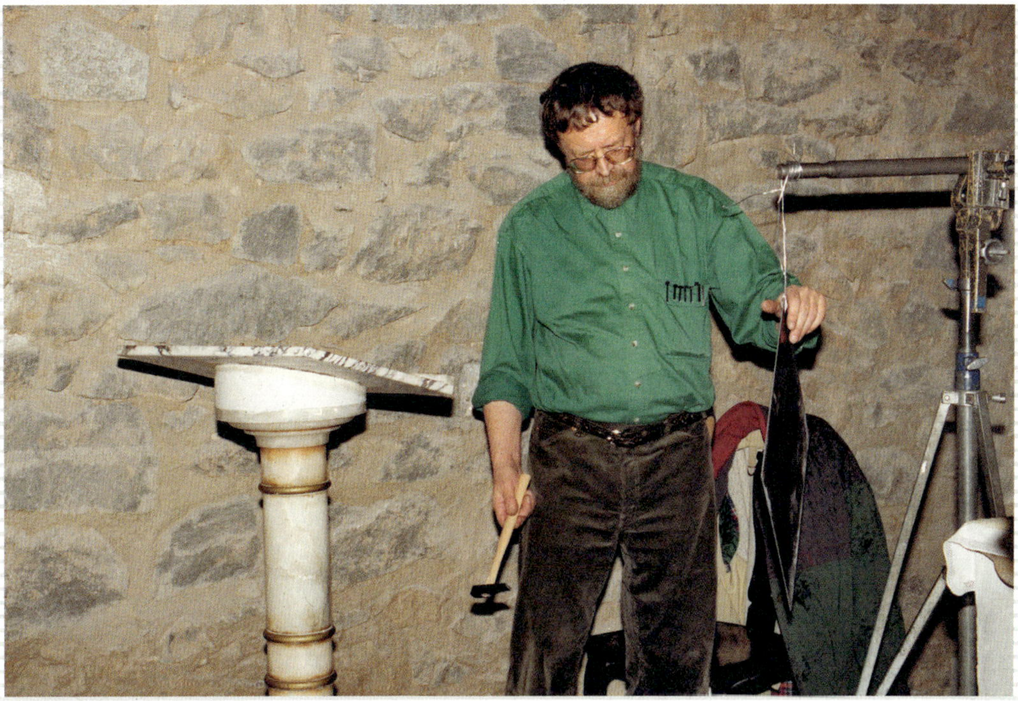

H.C. gives 30 smooth hammer strokes on a metal plate + rings Russian Zagorsk bells, saying: 'What time is it – is it what time – time is it what?'

Table placed in front of the altar.
Plaster on the table (plastic and thick paper on the floor).

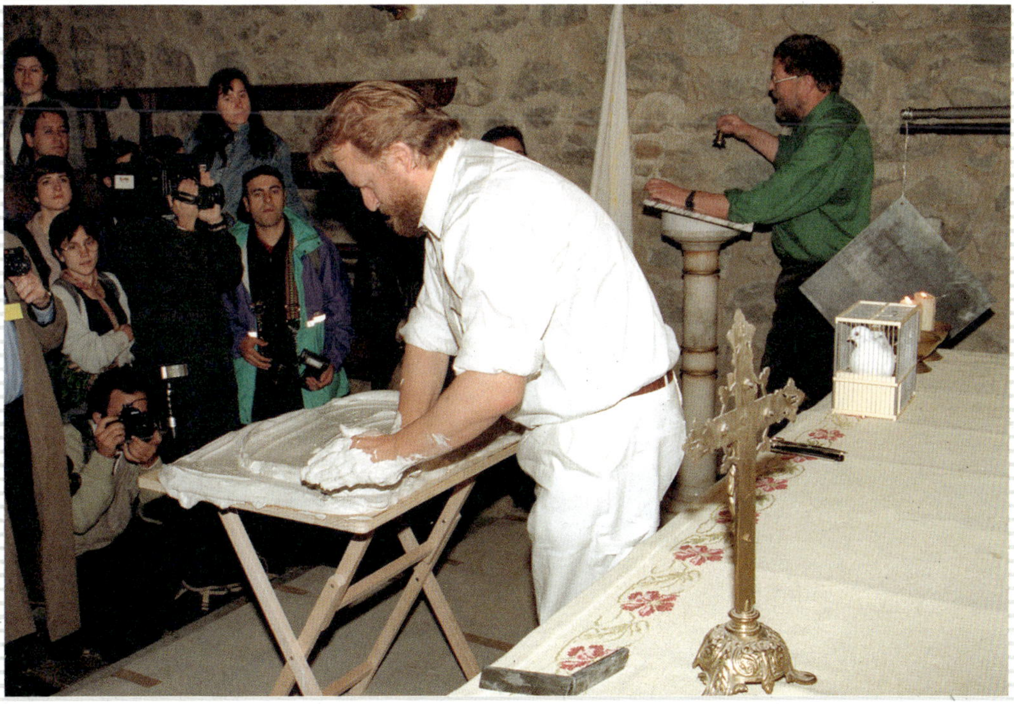

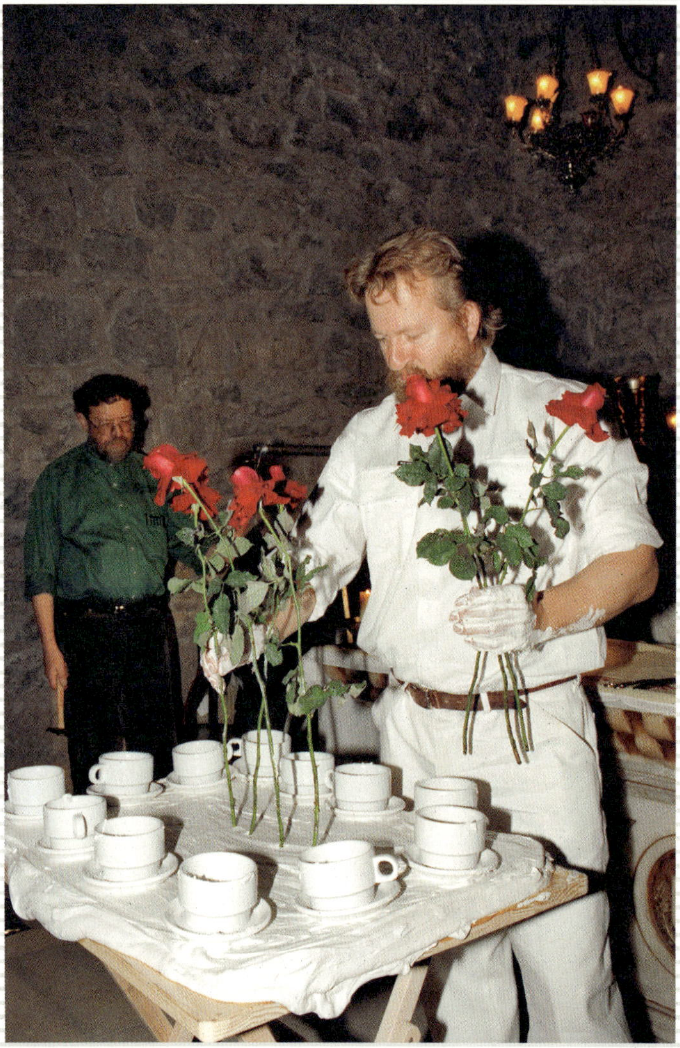

B.N. places 7 roses upright inside the plaster.
Places 12 coffee cups around the roses.
Pours water in the cups from a glass pitcher from 1m high.

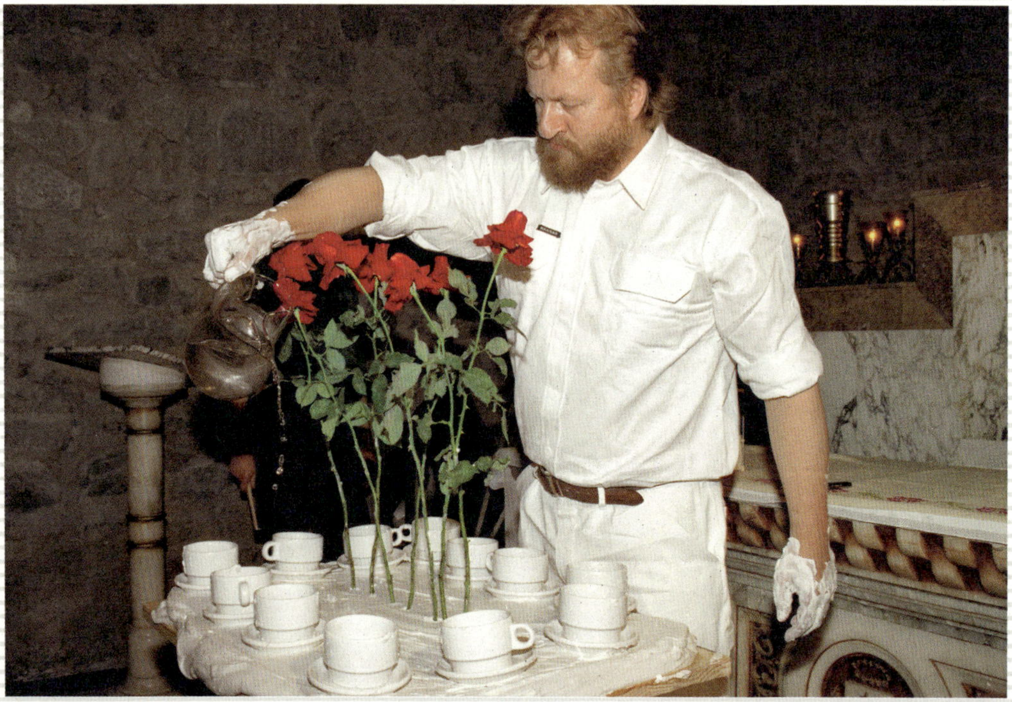

B.N. cuts his thumb and drips a drop of blood in every cup.
Then he cuts the roses and throws them to the audience.

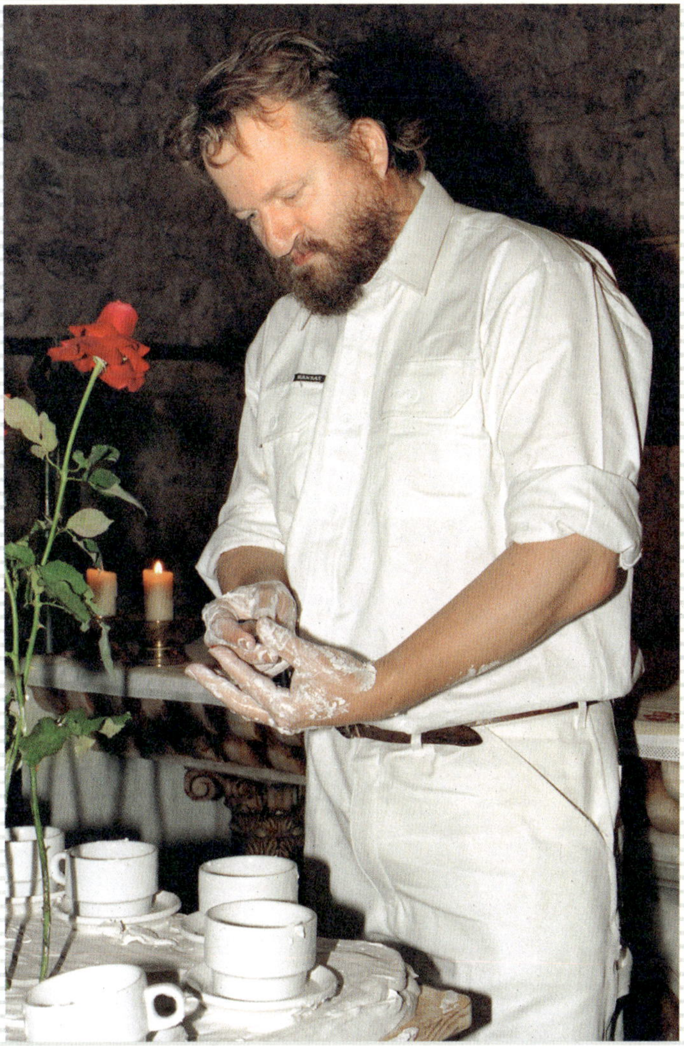

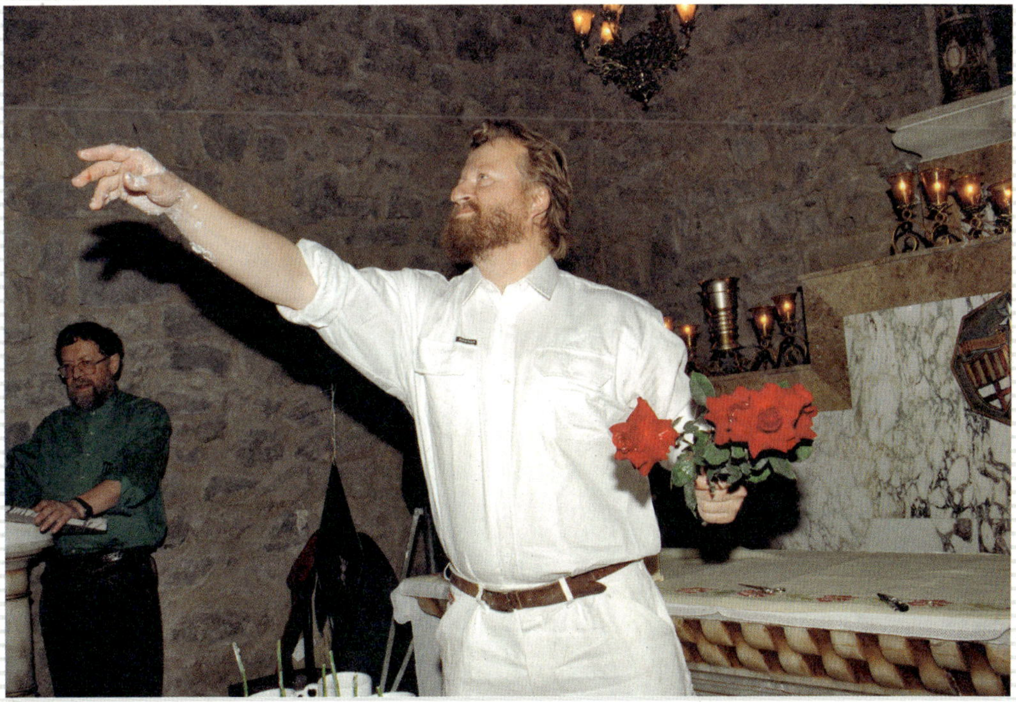

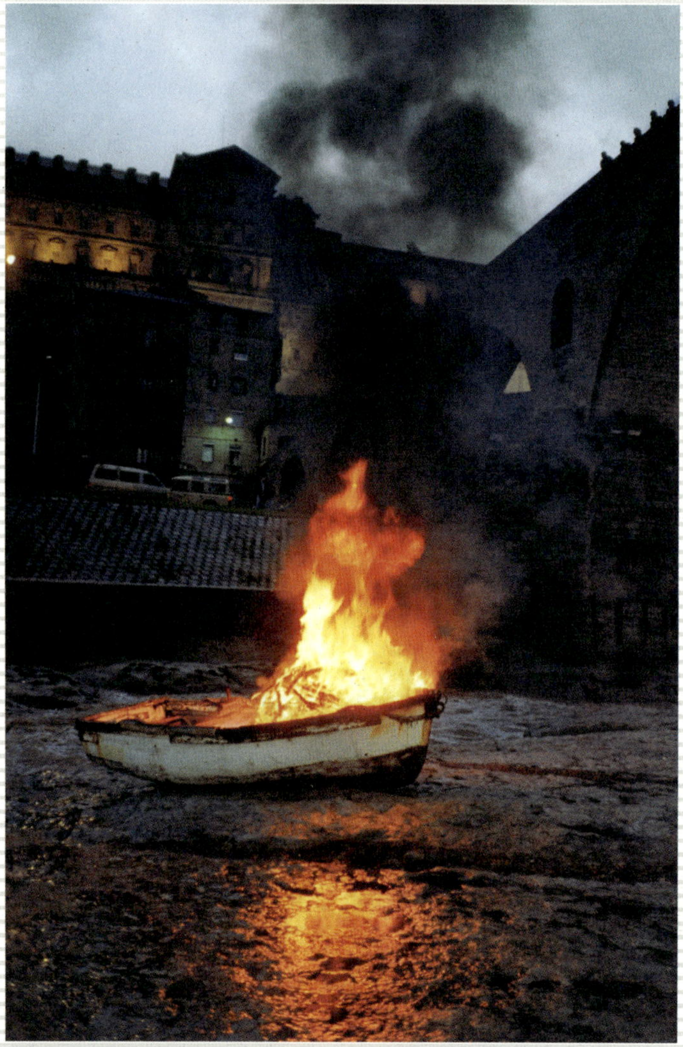

Fire on the boat.

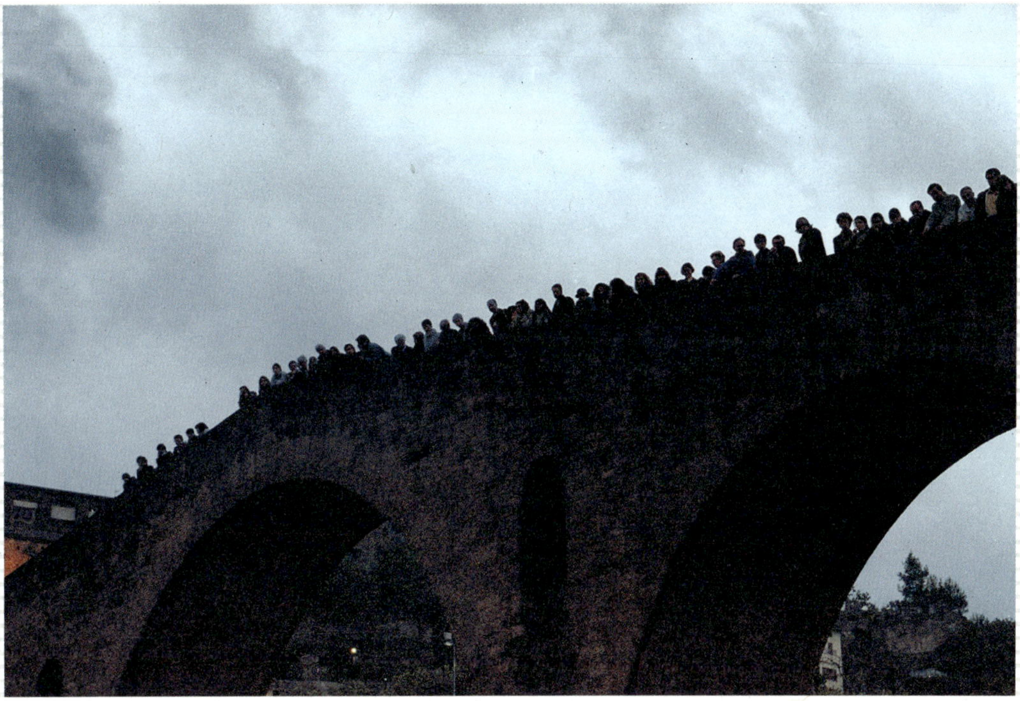

27 hammer strokes on metal (big hammer), intervals 1'.

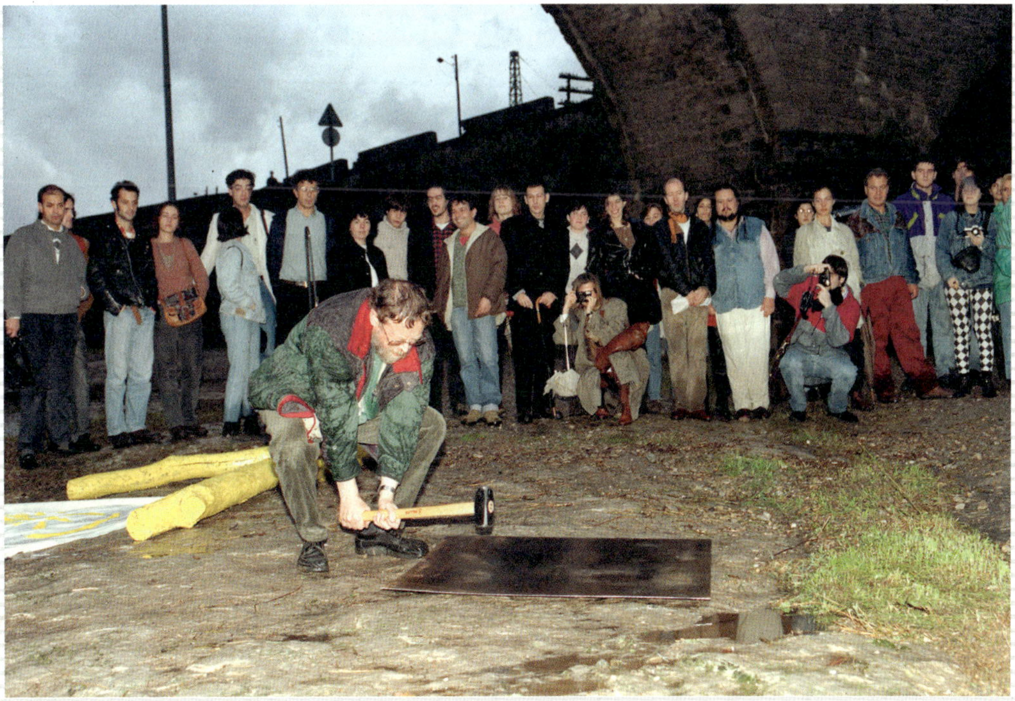

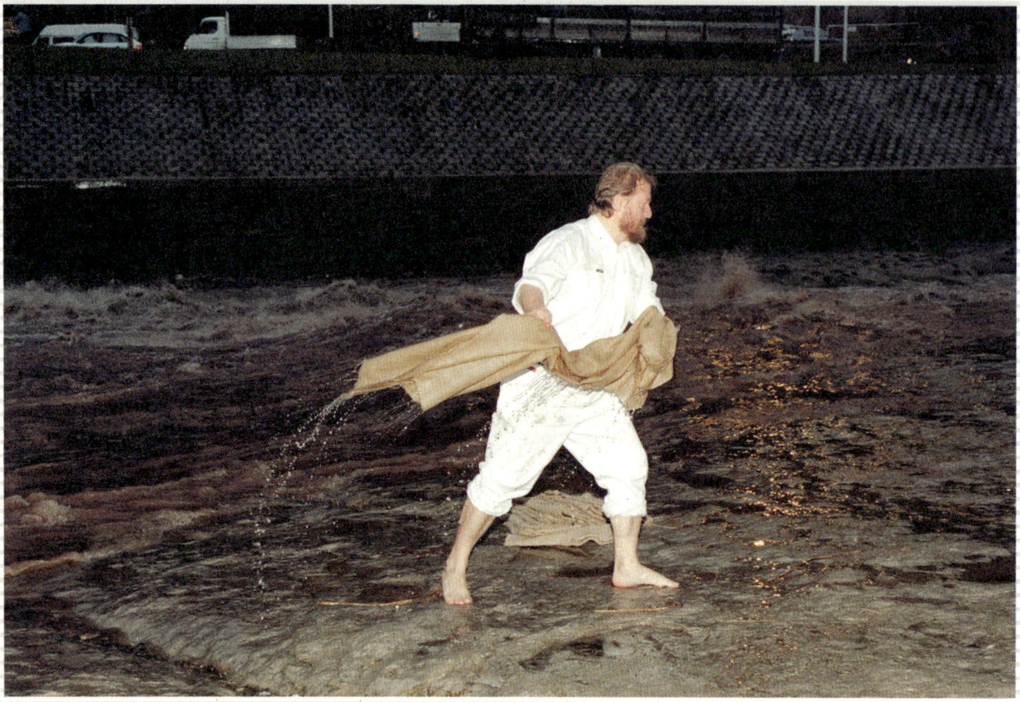

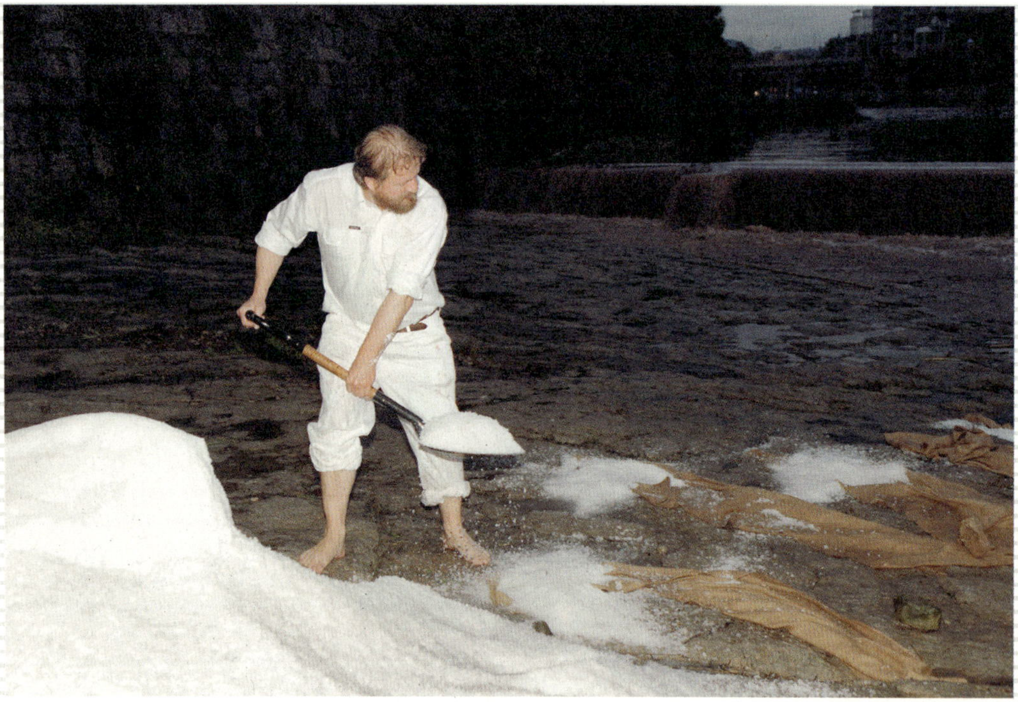

12 pieces of sackcloth are washed in the river
and smashed on the rocks.
Salt is thrown on them afterwards.

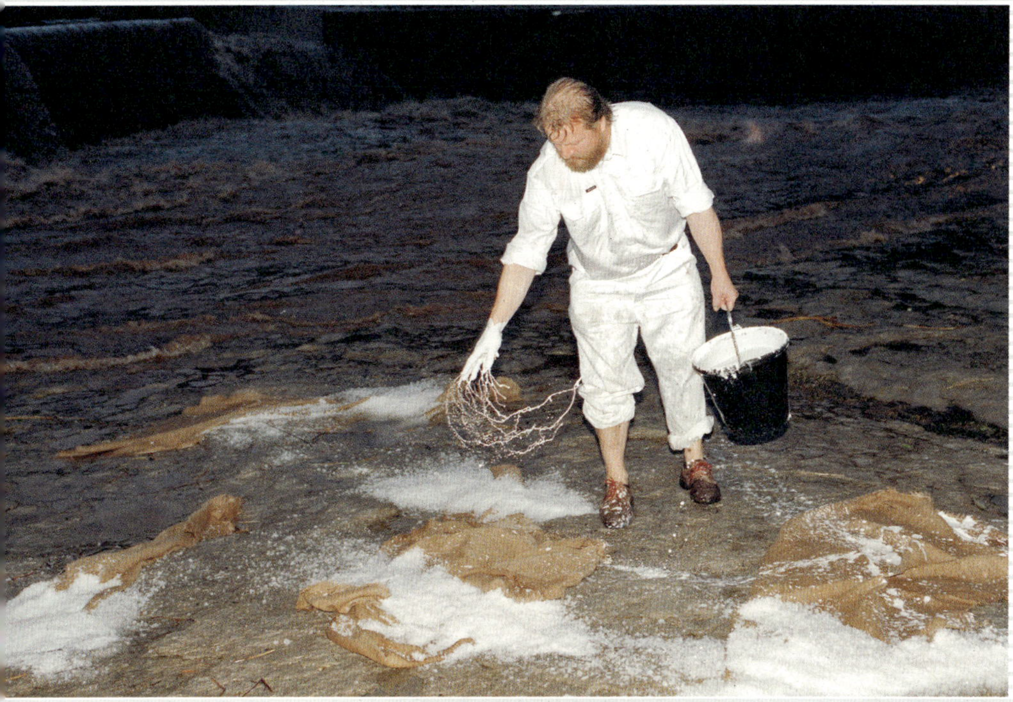

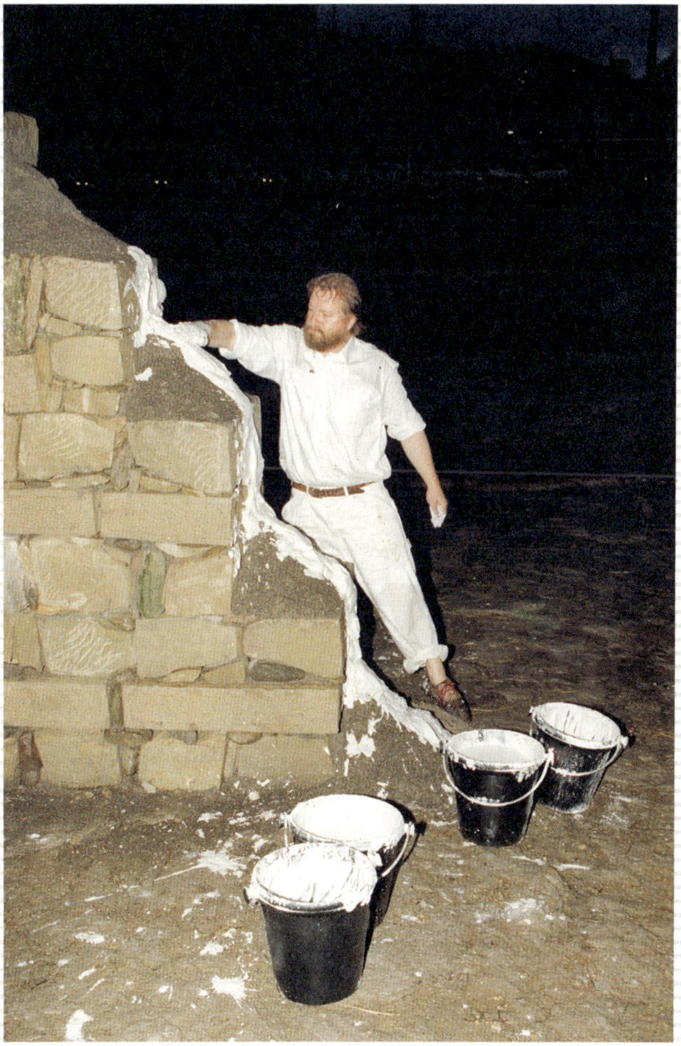

Jacob's ladder (staircase built of stone 1 day before).
A plaster ramp is built.

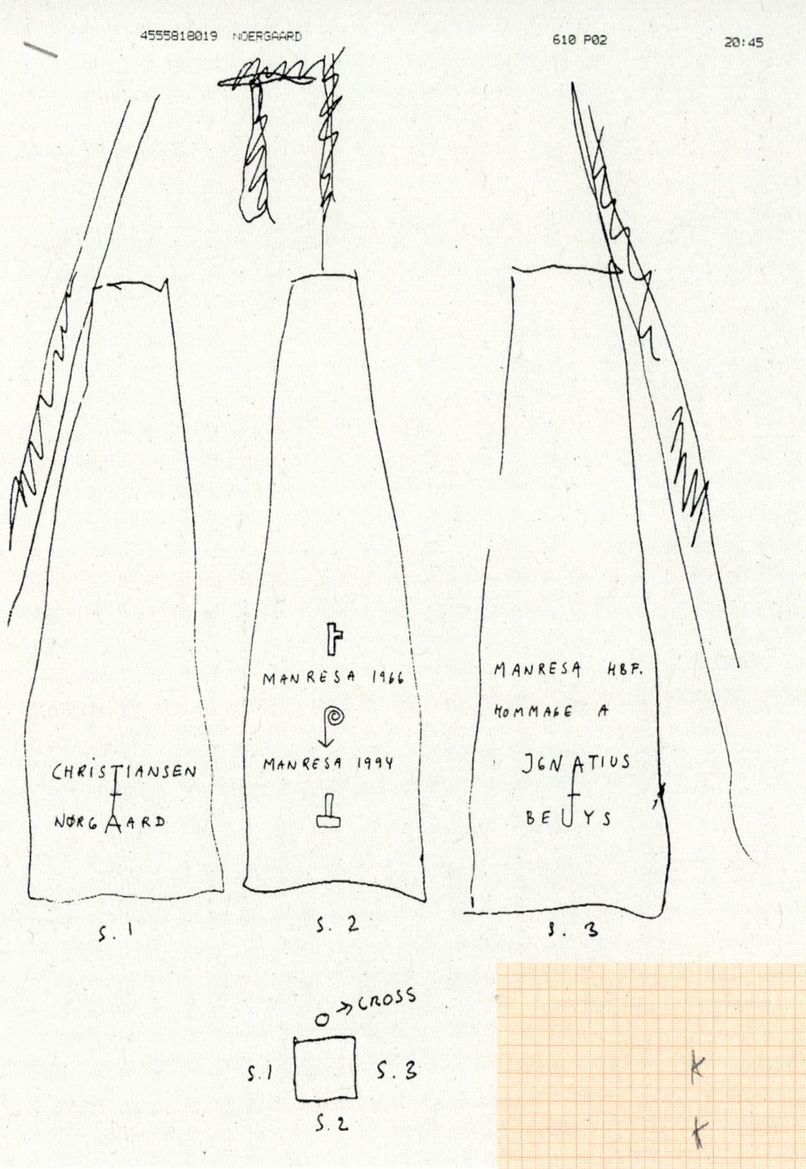

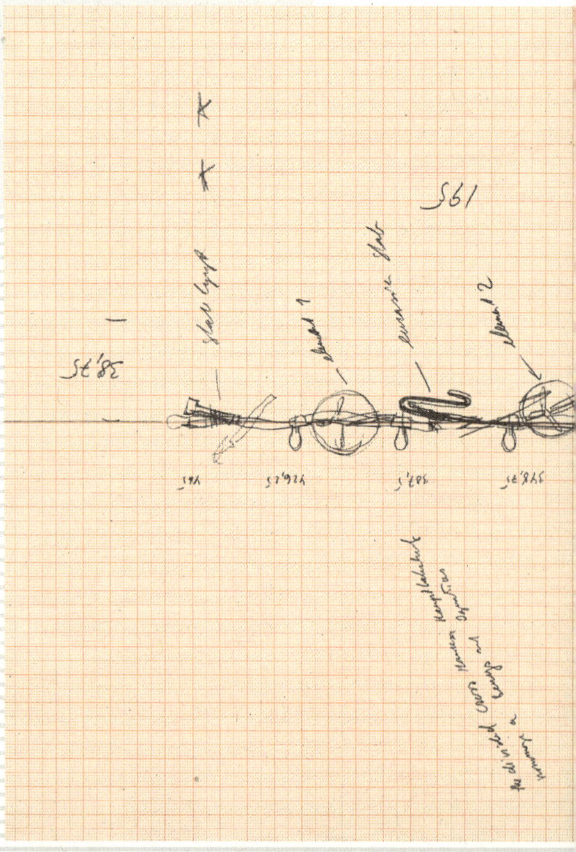

Bjørn Nørgaard, sketches for the cross, 1994.

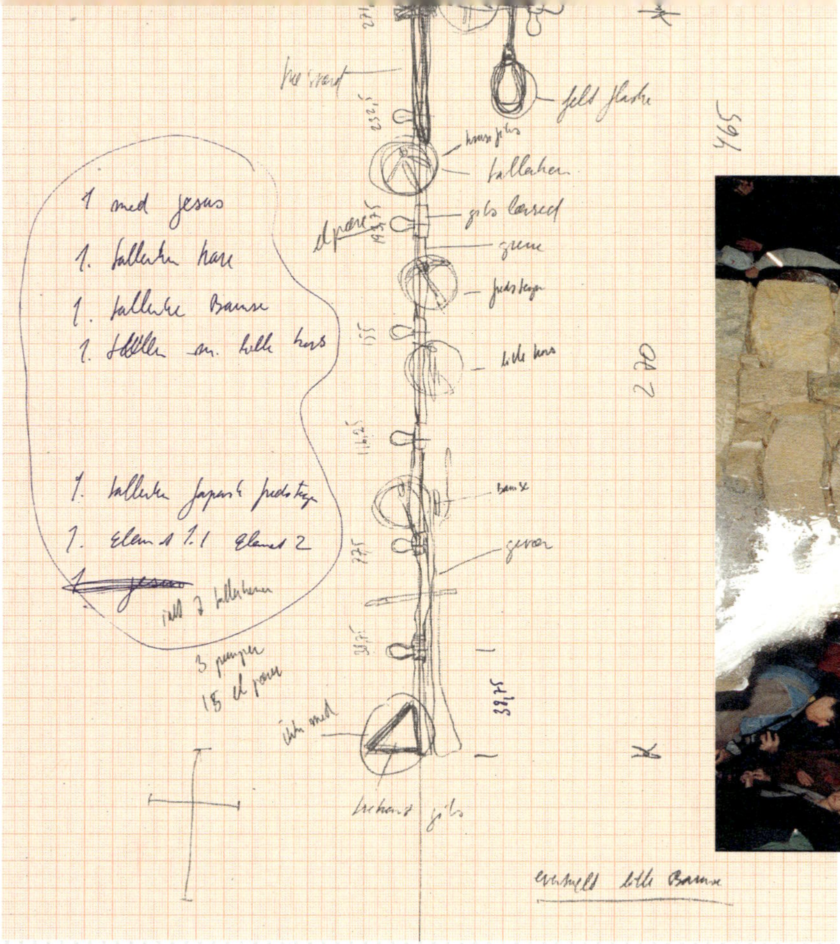

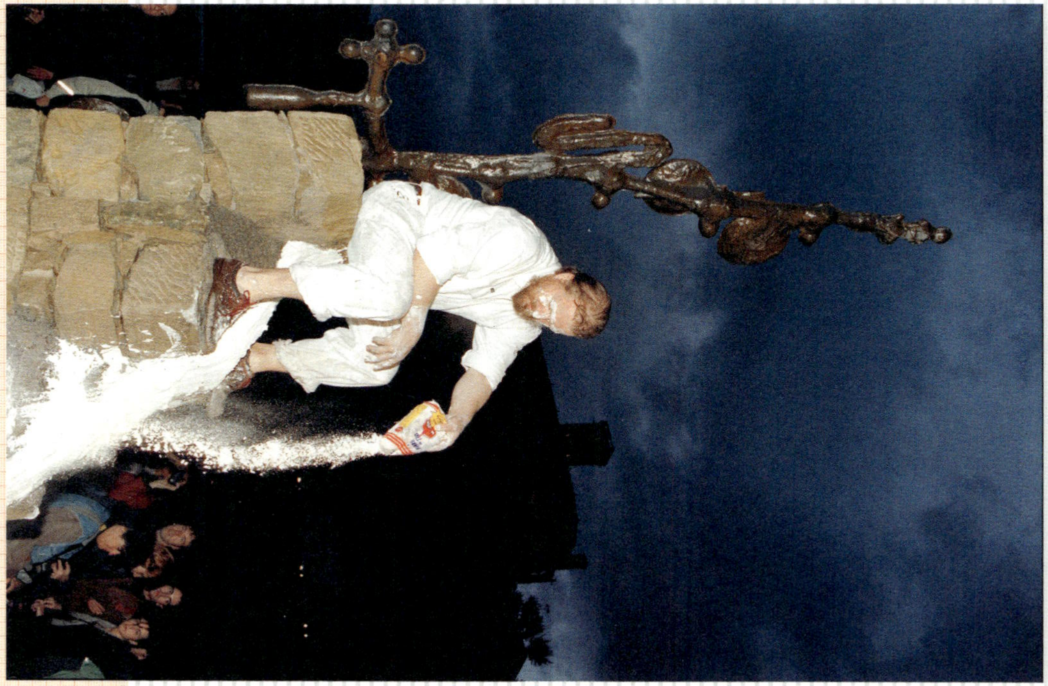

The iron cross is raised.
B.N. crawls to the top of the ladder and throws materials down the ramp (flour-salt-syrup-water-eggs).

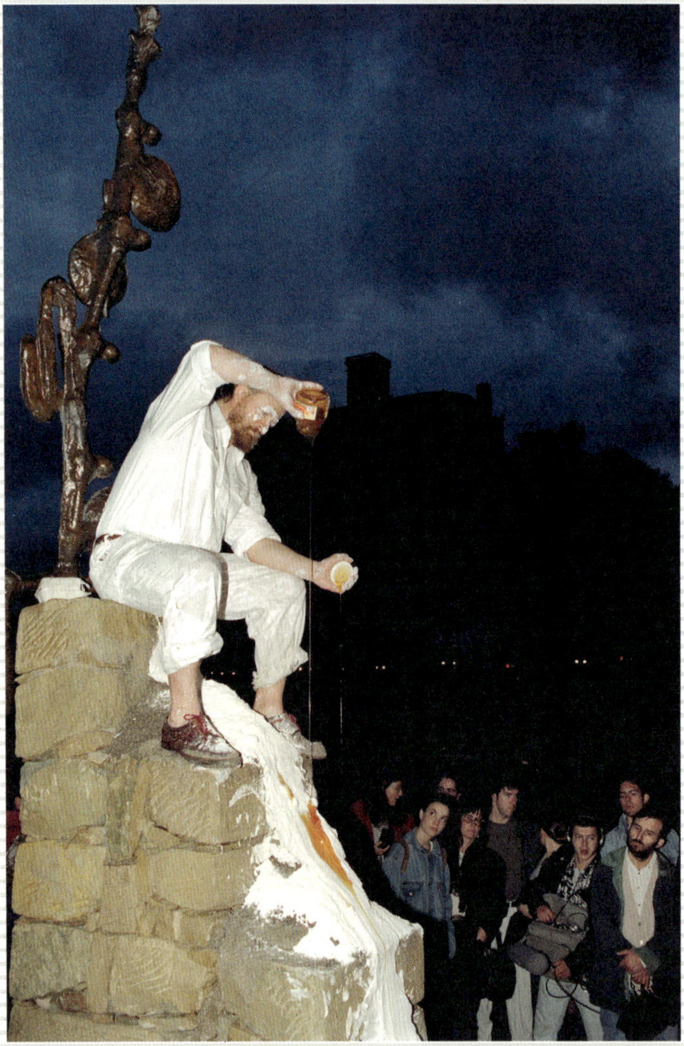

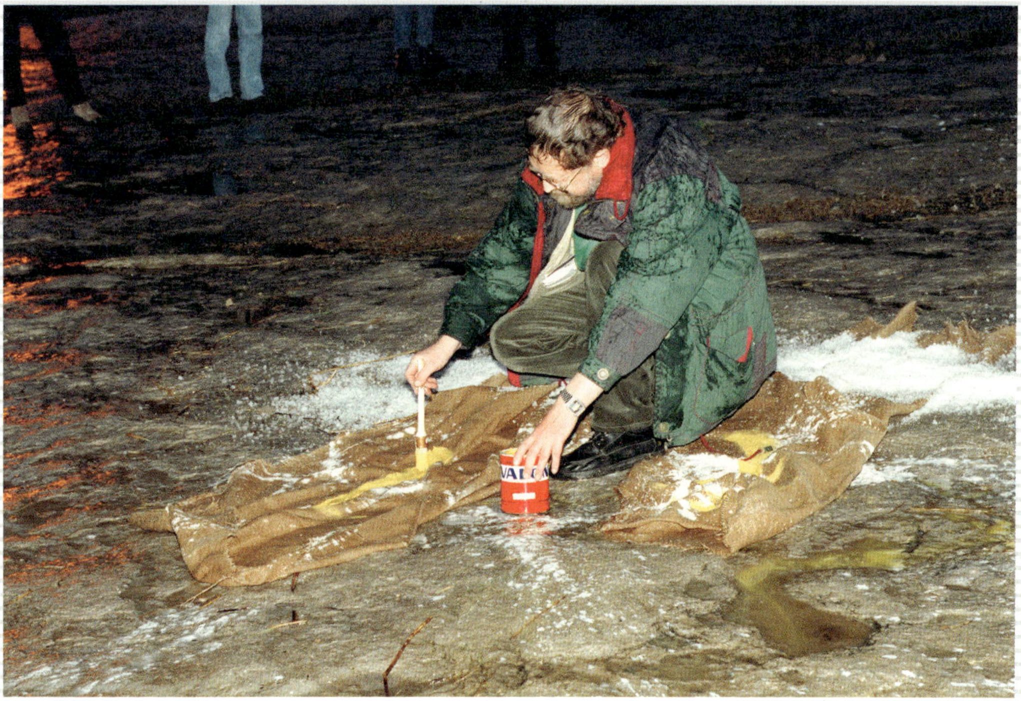

H.C. marks the sacks with the Japanese sign for peace in yellow.

2 fish are salted and bread is broken and placed on the sackcloth.

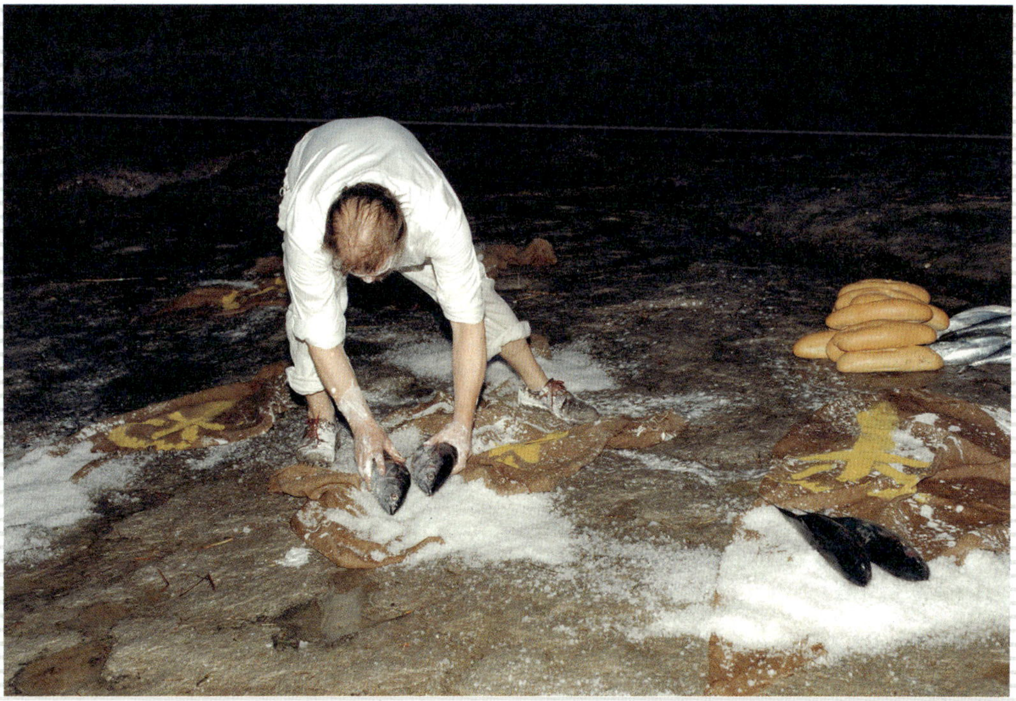

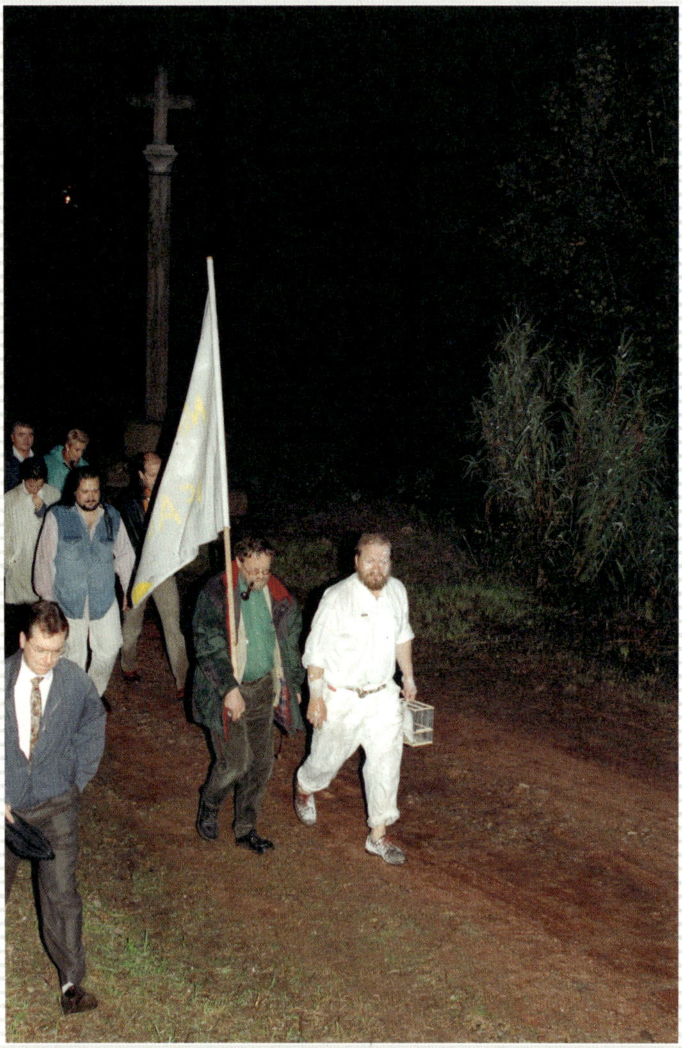

B.N. walks with the white dove.

H.C. plays the metal plate hanging on the flagstick with the hammer.

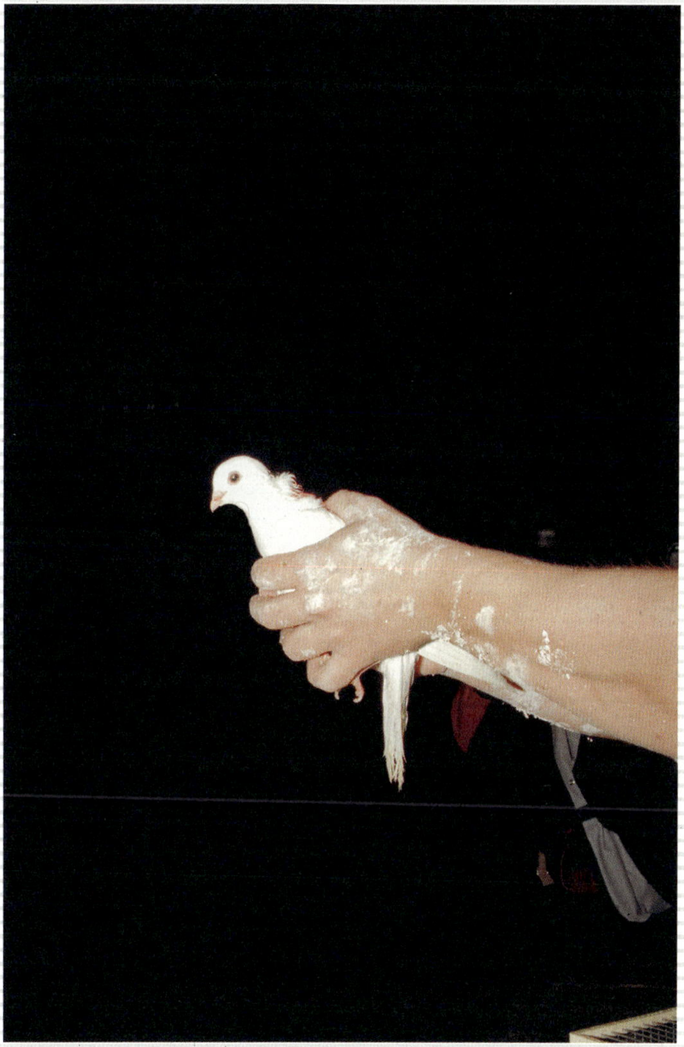

B.N. lets the dove go (fly).
H.C. throws the white flag down into the river.

FOURTH STATION ca. 20 min

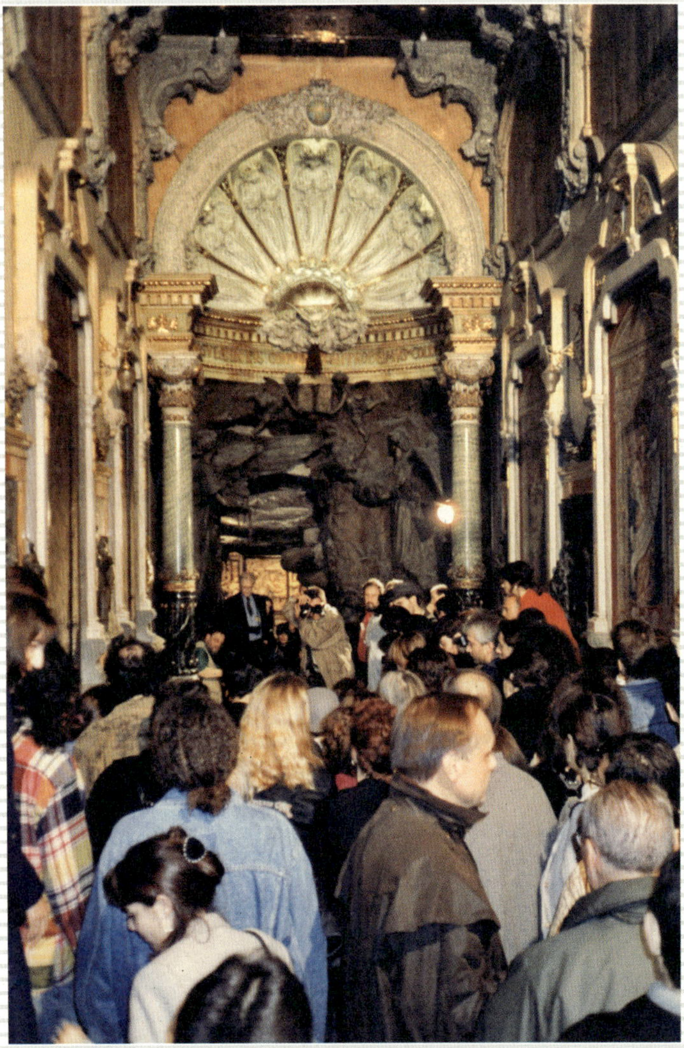

Stone Age Gramophone (from Denmark)
→ 'The peaceful green hammer'
3 times with the hammer:
'The stupid hammer'
'The clever hammer'
'The peaceful hammer'

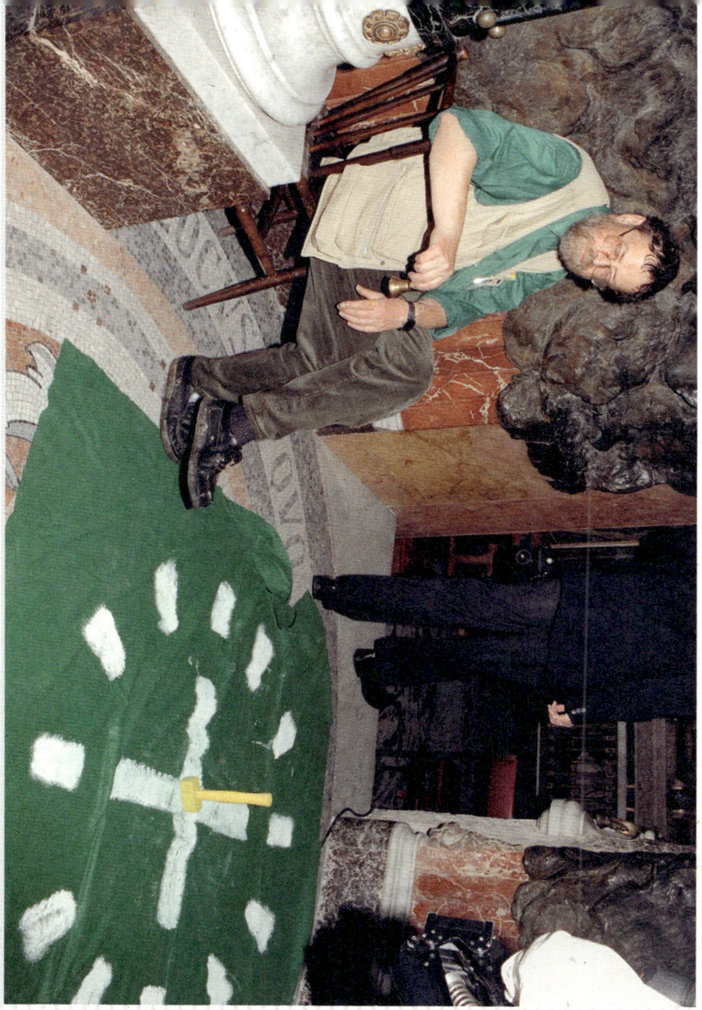

Sculptural Demonstration with the feet,
as performed in the first MANRESA action in 1966:
1. Walk on bottles | 2. Smashing bulbs | 3. Stamping on clay in flour | 4. Gliding in crystal soap | 5. Splashing in water | 6. Plaster feet

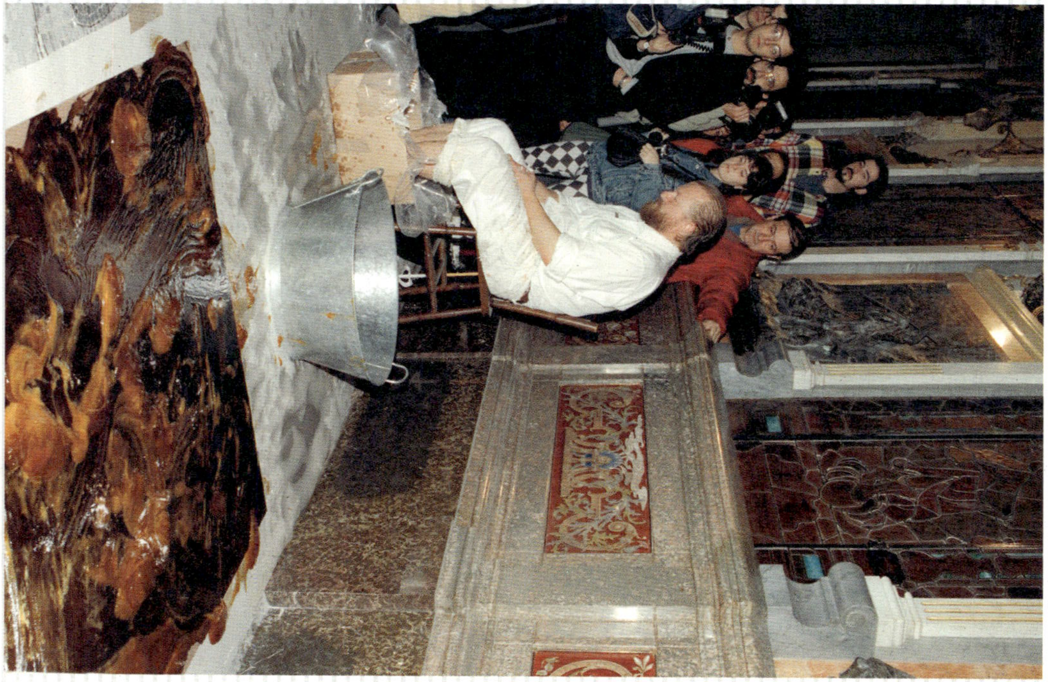

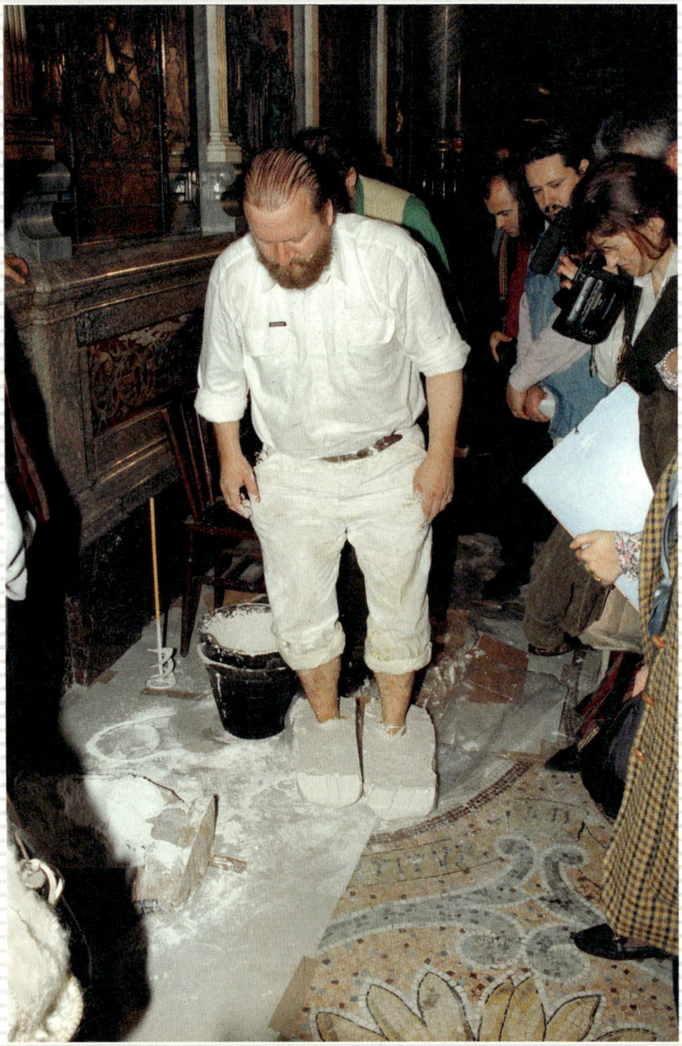

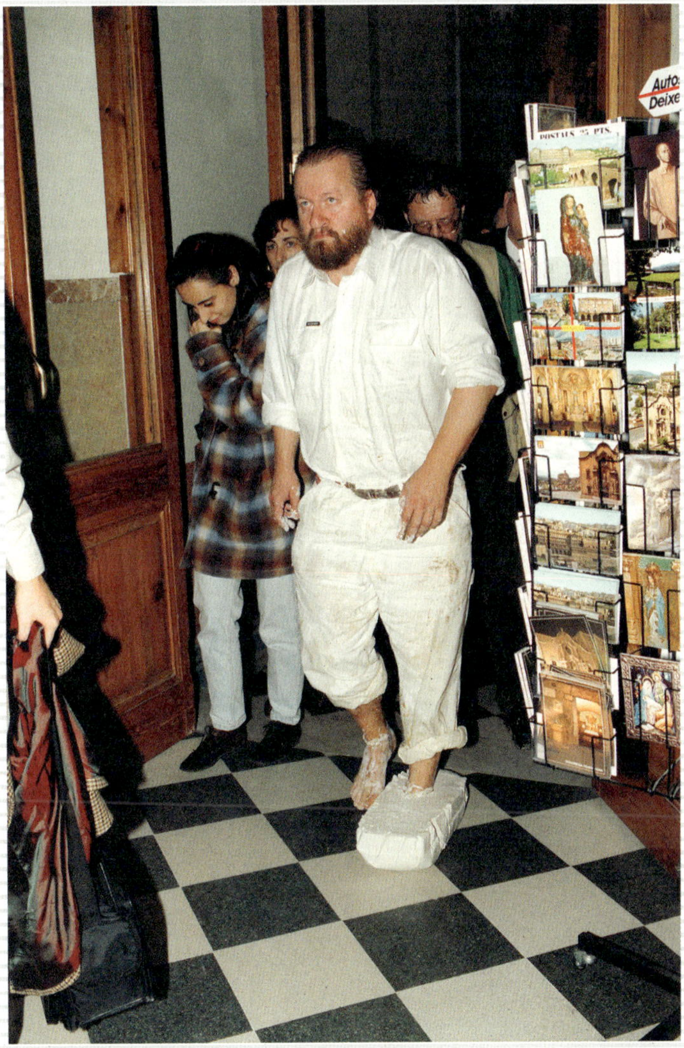

B.N. walking with plaster feet to the church room.
H.C. sharp sound.

FIFTH STATION ca. 60 min

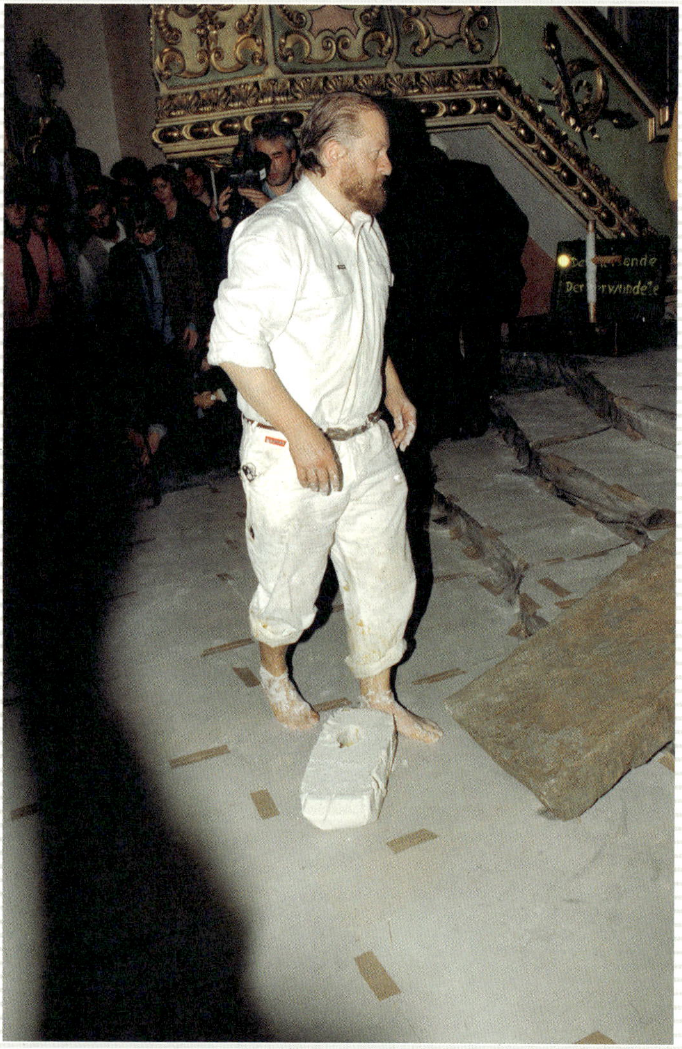

H.C. Sound from MANRESA 1966.

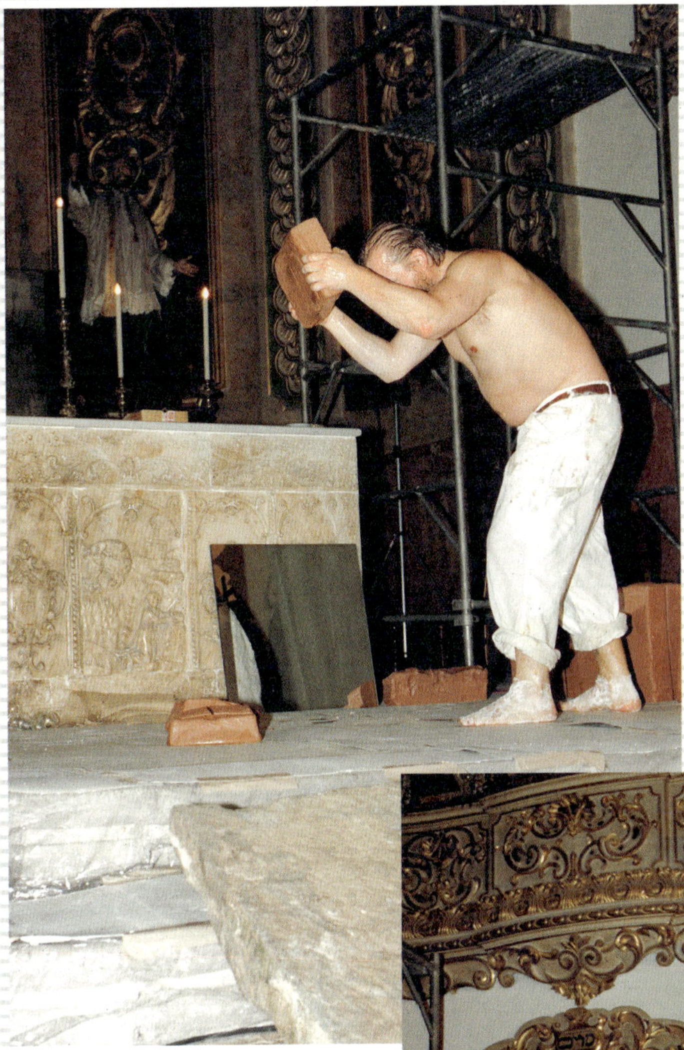

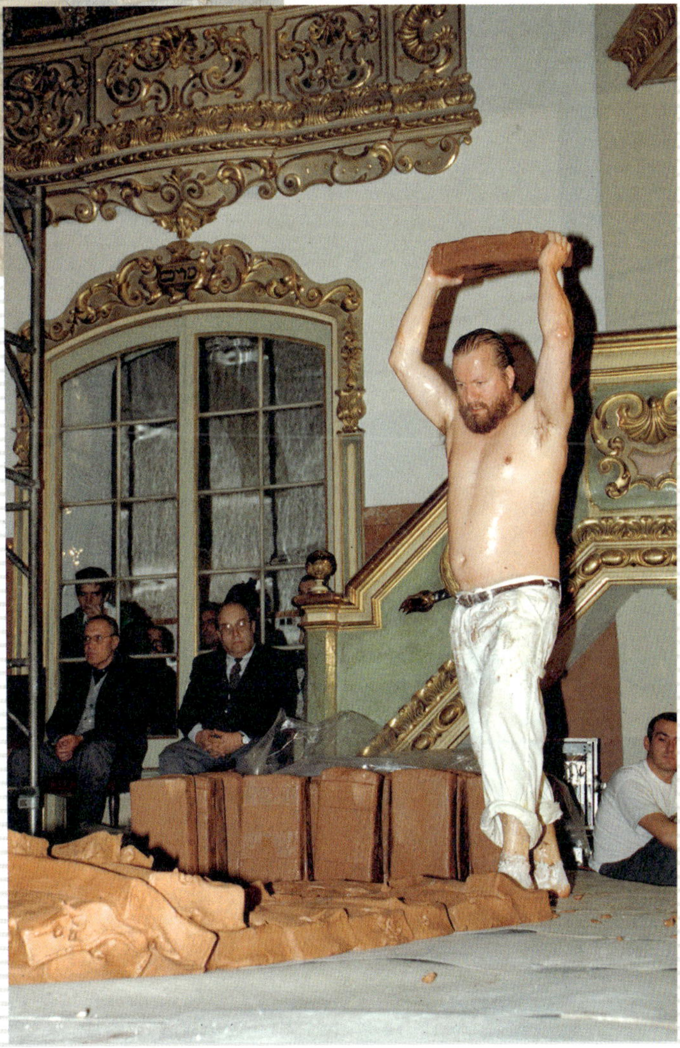

B.N. constructing the bed with clay,
electric bulbs and mirrors.

Save the nature
___use FLUXUS

Henning Christiansen

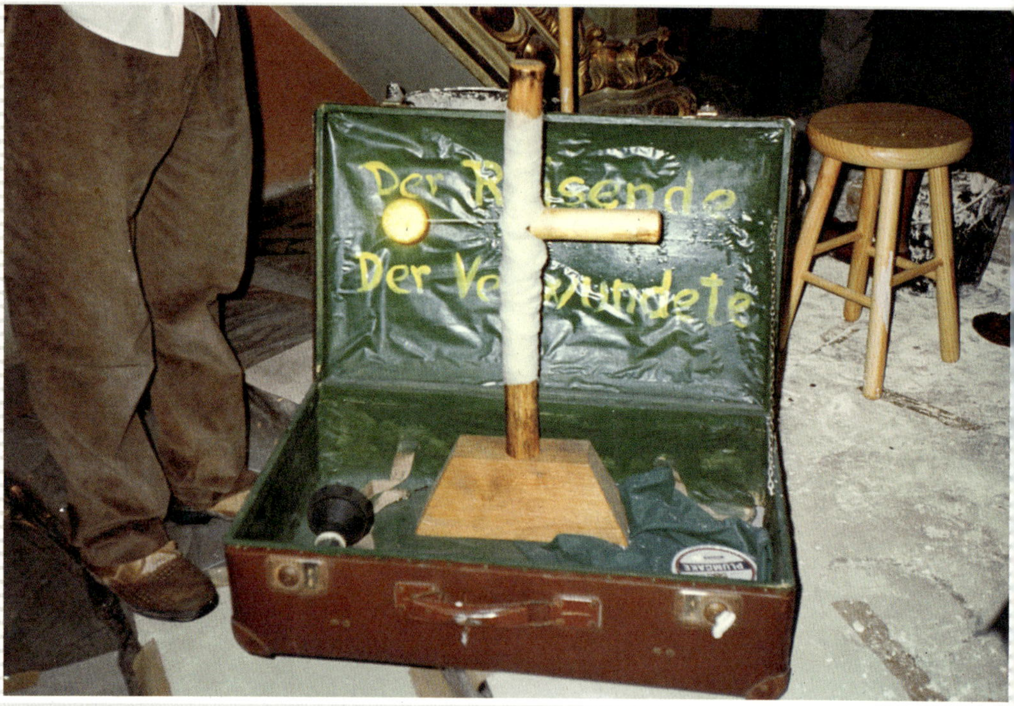

B.N. constructing the road to MANRESA in plaster.

Constructing the 12 disciples with gravel, panes of glass and eggs.

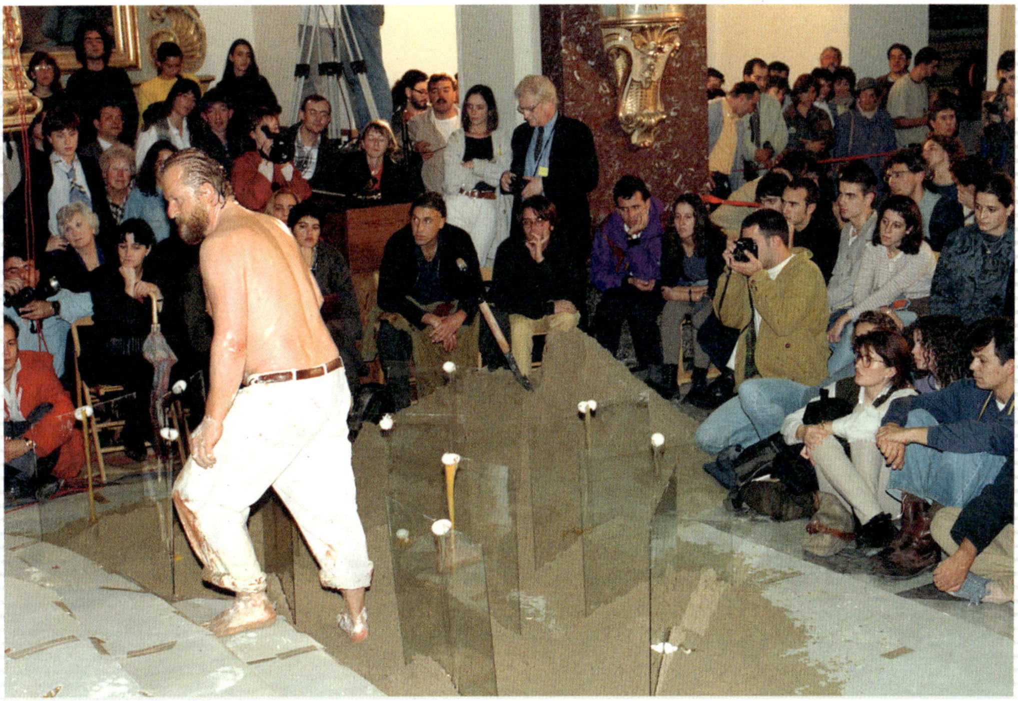

H.C.

I. Water from can in the bucket.

II. Show text 'Save the nature – use FLUXUS'.

III. Open the bag 'the divided cross'. Light on the cross.

IV. Counting-song. Bird whistle.

V. TIME reading.

VI. can – I can't.

VII. 8 bicycle pumps with clay.

VIII. Knocking-song.

IX. Show text 'Save the nature – use FLUXUS'.

X. Mentionable.

XI. Water Music – Old Russian bells of Zagorsk [Sergiyev Posad]. (30 min)

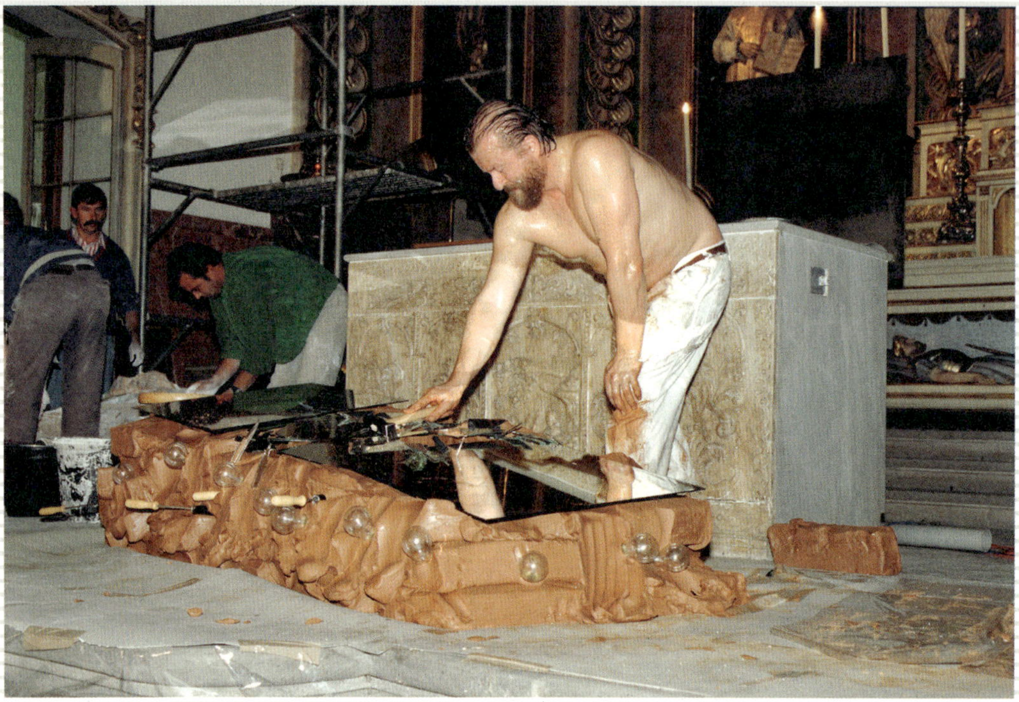

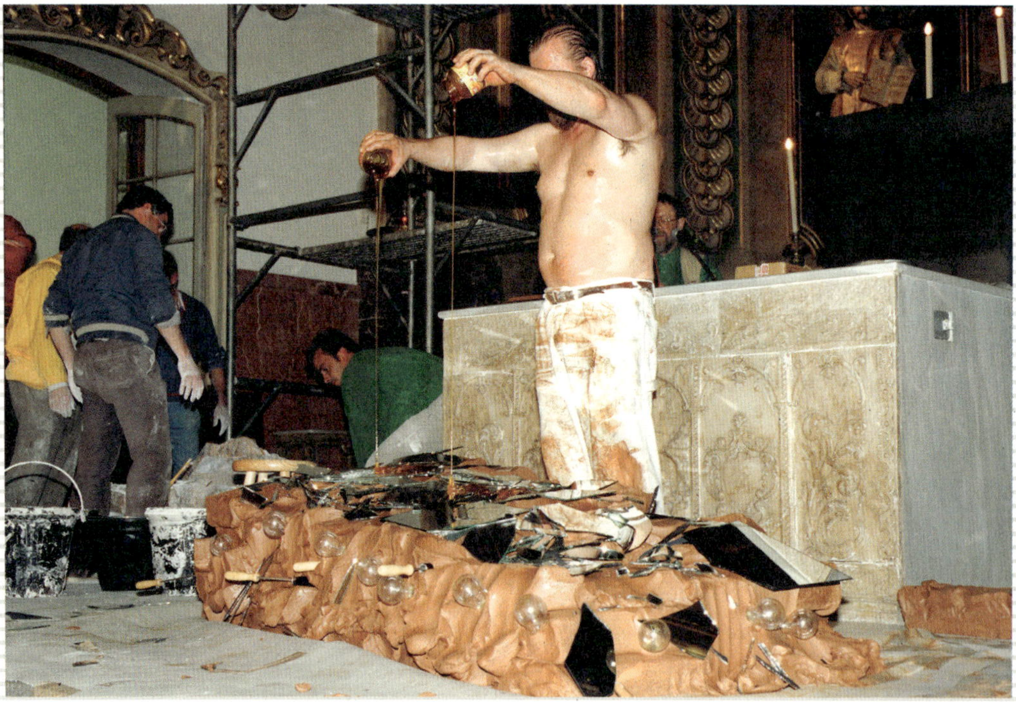

Smashing the mirrors and pouring syrup on them.

The deformation of the body with sackcloth and plaster.
Sleep - Dream - transformational vision.

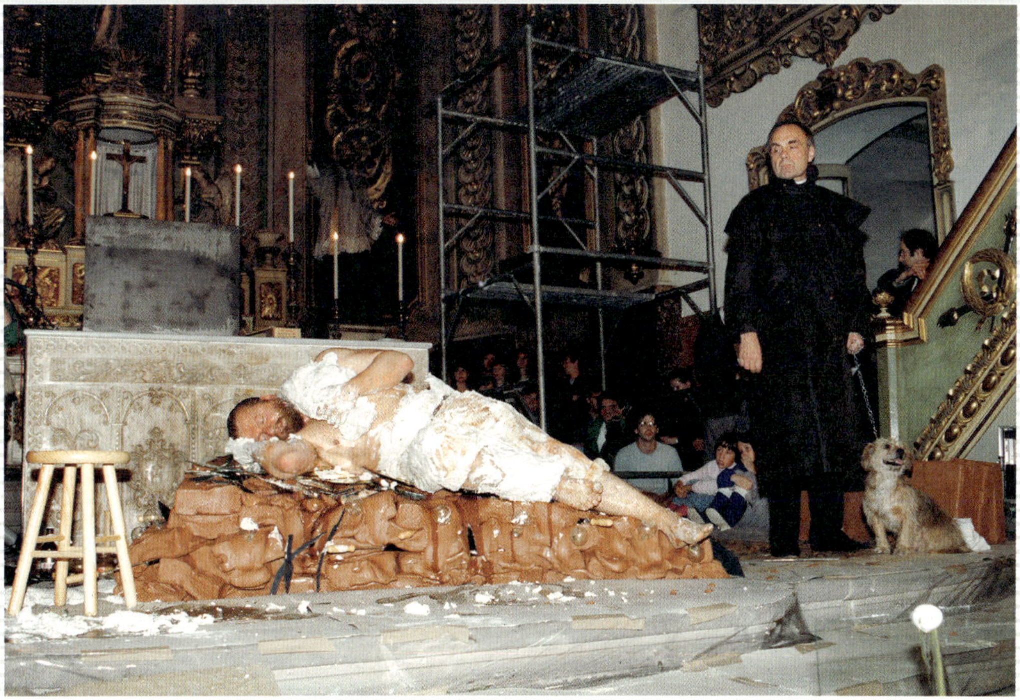

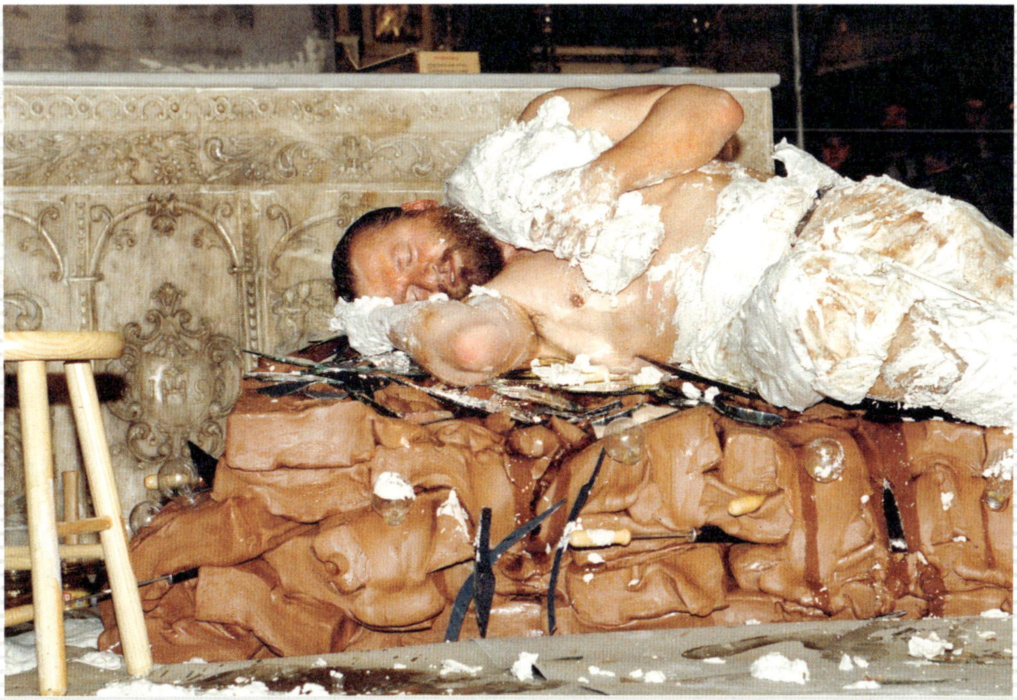

SIXTH STATION ca. 30 min

Fire at the fireplace.

Mennekes reads a text + H.C. interrupts with sounds.

B.N. gives the audience bread and fish.

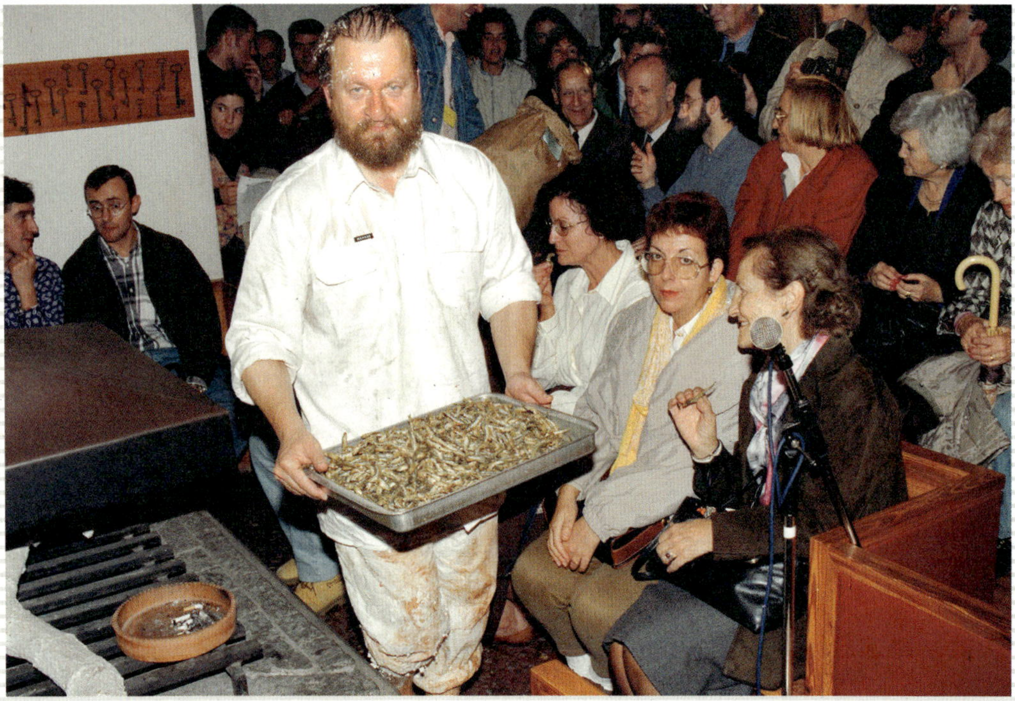

HENNING CHRISTIANSEN

REALITY MULTIPLIED BY THREE: FOUR EPISTLES ON JOSEPH BEUYS'S WORKING METHODS

A false interpretation (I) that is nevertheless neither incorrect nor unimportant

BEUYS'S WORK revolves around reality and poetry. The one extreme, reality, is starkly harsh, and the other, poetry, is like a delicate breath. The former can be demonstrated, leaving no one in doubt; the latter requires thought and insight. Beuys likes to speak of *Gegenraum* ('anti-' or 'counter space') and *Gegenzeit* ('anti-' or 'counter time'). He contrasts mathematics with anti-mathematics, chemistry with anti-chemistry, physics with anti-physics and, in keeping with these terms, nature with anti-nature. When he uses the words 'anti' and 'counter', he is in fact referring to humans themselves. These notions of 'anti' and 'counter' turn space into an experiential setting. Time becomes experiential time: matter becomes mind.

This notion of the 'opposite' of reality can be found in poetry in general, if we assume that imaginary reality is one side of the coin and material reality the other. Poetry is the most extreme, intense medium with which to make this happen. Poetry pushes things to a point where space and counter space or time and counter-time — to stay with Beuysian concepts — seem identical; and this provokes or rather forces us into dealing with the undeniably profound question: in which one does the real world truly reside?

Beuys's poetry grapples with the thin line between the worlds of poetry and material reality. He concentrates on both sides of the coin. And herein also lies the reason why it is so difficult to understand what he is trying to do. He brings the worlds of poetry and materiality together; at first glance they even appear to coexist perfectly. Beuys ultimately approaches the available material with his psychological non-existence — and this appears as a poetic existence.

Here is a good example: Beuys has used chocolate as a material in a long series of works. Brown chocolate, which he paints exactly the same colour as the original. The line between the real and painted chocolate can only be seen by looking very closely. Material and artistic method coincide before our very eyes. But there is a gap between the two: one side of the coin (material) is chocolate that can be eaten and the other (artistic method) is paint, a traditional art medium. All of Beuys's earliest works make use of similar working methods to achieve both realities. They also give us a glimpse of where to look for constants in his work.

A false interpretation (II) that is nevertheless neither incorrect nor unimportant

Beuys became known as a graphic artist and sculptor and later as a 'material poet' and action artist (i.e. happenings or demonstrations). In his sculptures made of wood, slate, stone, bronze, steel or iron, we realise in retrospect something significant; namely, that he allows materials to retain their properties. The art he designs is based on the laws that the material is subject to. This is noteworthy because an artist's treatment of their material presupposes a conscious or unconscious attitude towards it. What is added is hardly visible and is harmonious, both artistically and materially. The term 'material properties' is heavily loaded, and in Beuys's case leads us completely astray: he does not work with wood because of its tendency to splinter, but uses wood to express the notion of splintering. In the same way, he uses slate for the concept of stacking, stone for compact volume, bronze for a skin-like texture and steel for a polished surface. These connections are not all purely related to craftmanship, but also to the meaning of abstract motifs. To express Christ's sacrifice on the cross (Beuys's early work features many carved crucifixes), he uses wood — a material that splinters.

As I said above, this is all my interpretation, but I do not think I am entirely wrong, seeing it from the point of view of Beuys's earliest works and how his art has developed. But that is not all. While these observations only consider a few specific aspects of his works, they are undoubtedly some of the most important and consistent ones. Even if he has not completely moved away from drawing and sculpture, Beuys is primarily regarded as a 'material poet' and action artist. This is well-suited to his intentions of working with the extreme poles of reality.

Beuys has created hundreds of 'objects' over time. However, the term 'object' does not really suit them because material properties are an essential part of what Beuys wants to express. He does not focus on the 'object' aspect of his work with materials — but on their transformation. He emphasises the flipping of the coin, turning poetic reality face up.

Another wrong interpretation (III) that is nevertheless not insignificant and not unreliable

Beuys treads the thin line between two realities, with artistic confidence and an obstinate, finely-honed consistency. His 'objects' are mostly image-like in nature. He still makes a relatively large number of additions and changes. An example of this is his clay sculpture, *Snow-Covered Rider* from 1958. The figure can be made out even though it is not directly visible. The memory of a figure presents itself and tries to introduce us to the creative process of sculpture, a well-known discipline that we are very familiar with. Sculpture as a discipline is an existing poetic reality, an age-old medium with which we can comprehend psychological existence through material properties. For as long as it is possible to map Beuys's ideas of images and sculpture onto traditional reception models, it will also be possible to misunderstand his works. In any case, in the above example, it is easy to draw conclusions that are slightly askew. Either we overlook the gauze covering the figure because we do not know how to read it; or we understand it as the essential part of the sculpture, but are then in a similar position to that of the chocolate mentioned above, as an example of two realities jostling for space and as a reflection of the basic principles of Beuys's work.

Beuys's development as an artist did not occur as quickly as we have jumped from one example to another here. Over time, he has had to push aside many things that can be loosely described as artistic conventions, which might obstruct an understanding of his work before he mastered what very few other German artists did: the art of the action.

Another false interpretation (IV) that is nevertheless not disingenuous or insignificant.

'Demonstrations' — the term Beuys preferred to describe his own happening-like activities — comprised objects and elements of movement, time and sound. These could be subsumed under the category of kinetic art, except that works of this kind exclude humans. The human, as stated in the introduction, is regarded by Beuys as a psychological space, the meaningful side of the coin — as represented by 'anti' and 'opposite'.

Therefore, Beuys is following a consistent line when, to make use of psychological reality, he makes use of humans to achieve an invisible overlap of the two realities in the strongest way possible: because both realities are present in humans, where they are anyway identical. His 'demonstrations' are not specifically a discipline of theatre; they are performances, of anything, by humans. They themselves are 'objects', the subject of poetry, created by the poet himself.

What's more, if we consider Beuys's latest phase, it is clear that he was trying to get past the demonstration. When asked about the founding of his party — in particular what it had to do with his work as an artist — he said that it was a misunderstanding not to see his party as a work of art. Because that was what he intended it to be, just like his work as a professor at the art academy or any other activity he carried out. (For example, he very consciously wrote his own biography with exactly the same view — as a work of art).

Here we reach a point that can be compared to Malevich's white cross on a white background, from 1927, thus taking painting to its utmost extreme. The struggle or war between the material and spiritual ideas of humanity is something Joseph Beuys and Ignacio de Loyola shared in their will to pave the way for peaceful, dynamic humans.

The halved cross — the two realities of humans — and *Element 3 — I am flying to you too, MANRESA*.

Manuscript written in 1968.
Henning Christiansen Archive, Møn.

FRIEDHELM MENNEKES, S. J.

I AM FLYING TO YOU TOO, MANRESA

JOSEPH BEUYS (1921–1986) strived to connect art with life. This concept was at the heart of his work. His oeuvre succeeded in broadening perspectives of what art is. One example of this is the Fluxus demonstration MANRESA in 1966 (from now on referred to as MANRESA). With characteristic idiosyncrasy, Beuys performed this work on 15 December at the Schmela Gallery in Düsseldorf together with two Danish artists, the composer Henning Christiansen and the sculptor Bjørn Nørgaard. Crisis, illness and self-healing processes were themes explored in the action and whose importance went far beyond a single art action. For Beuys, these were the most important themes in his art throughout his life. MANRESA continued to make an impression in two additional performances after Beuys's death.

Twice after the original event in 1966, the MANRESA action was spectacularly 'expanded': first on 21 February 1991 at the Kunst-Station Sankt Peter in Cologne (from now on referred to as *Manresa '91*) and then on 4 November 1994 in the Catalan city of Manresa (referred to as *Manresa Hbf*). Neither event was an imitation; they were both free re-enactments inspired by the spirit of the original. Both were initiated by Henning Christiansen and Bjørn Nørgaard, taking place in Cologne on the occasion of the 500th anniversary of the birth of Ignatius of Loyola (1491–1556) and in Catalonia 'in the beautiful valley of Manresa', as it is called in a drawing for Fluxus demonstration.[1]

The MANRESA re-enactment in 1991

In 1991, and after Beuys's death in 1986, the 500th anniversary of Ignatius's birth was the occasion for a partial re-enactment of the MANRESA action by Henning Christiansen and Bjørn Nørgaard. Twenty-five years after the original performance, the two organised a Fluxus event again in the crowded Kunst-Station Sankt Peter in Cologne: MANRESA developed into *Manresa '91*. In addition to music compositions by Christiansen and 'material actions' by Nørgaard, the tape recording originally spoken by Beuys was also part of the re-enactment. In an accompanying exhibition, almost all of the drawings, photos and materials of the action that were still available or newly discovered were on display as originals or copies.[2]

This exhibition, which attracted attention far beyond Cologne, initiated many leads to hitherto completely unknown documents. The number of photographs alone which were known up till then increased tenfold. But the number of drawings of the action — called *Partituren* (scores) — also doubled because an entirely new network of connections emerged. As a result, the action, whose framework had only been known imprecisely up until then, could be described anew and its importance re-evaluated.[3]

The re-enactment in *Manresa Hbf*

In 1994, three years after the Cologne performance, the composer Henning Christiansen and the sculptor Bjørn Nørgaard organised a new edition of the Fluxus demonstration, MANRESA, in the town of Manresa helped by the great effort and support of others.[4] Participants included the internationally renowned art curator Harald Szeemann, the French musician Christophe Charles and myself. The title of this major event was: *Manresa Hauptbahnhof* (Manresa, Central Station).[5] The city's art historian Pilar Parcerisas, known from her numerous exhibitions in Barcelona, curated the action. For her, Manresa was 'a site with special conditions, an energy hub where the waters of the River Cardener and the light from Montserrat symbolically intersect. It is a sacred mountain whose radiance, in the course of its history, has given rise to intuitions of great importance; enlightenment that has been able to completely change people and their world.'[6]

The action itself, which was both a sequence of images of a pilgrimage of kind and an art trip, took place on 4 November 1994 in the Cardener valley at two prominent locations: below the city on both riverbanks and the old bridge. It started at the RENFE train station on the south-eastern riverbank, which was renamed *Manresa Hauptbahnhof* for the event, and the first stop was at the nearby chapel. The path of the action then led up the rocky shore and continued over the Roman bridge to Santa Cova (the Holy Cave where Ignatius had carried out his spiritual exercises) and the adjacent Ignatius Church, then on to the Centre for Spirituality; it ended with a monographic exhibition on Beuys's MANRESA Fluxus demonstration. The individual 'stations' were:

Station I:
Nostra Senyora de la Guia Shrine

The hermitage is a small chapel above the station behind the railway tracks on a small bank. It was packed with people. The six performers who took part in the action entered the room: the Danish artists Henning Christiansen and Bjørn Nørgaard, the French musician Christophe Charles, the Swiss curator Harald Szeemann, myself, from Germany, and the Barcelona-based curator Pilar Parcerisas, who was born in Manresa. In front of the bare altar was a small table (60 × 90 × 78 cm). The action began when Bjørn Nørgaard set the table with twelve white cups for an evening of discussion. In the middle, he arranged seven roses in an upright row, and he then aimed water into the cups from a glass jug at a height of about one metre. After that, he pierced his fingers with needles and let a pinprick of blood fall into each cup. He cut the long-stemmed roses one by one with a knife and threw them to the people standing in the small church. These actions commemorated the blood of the Passion, Joseph Beuys's rose, which he always kept on the lectern during his artist's lectures, and the Last Supper. Henning Christiansen made a 15-minute-long musical accompaniment to this action, with three times twelve light taps with a hammer on metal plates and by sounding liturgical bells from a Russian monastery. At the same time, he called out in the room: 'What time is it — is it what time — time is it what?' After a short silence, the two performers stepped out in front of the church. There they heaved a five-metre Ignatius Halved Cross onto their shoulders. Bjørn Nørgaard had brought it with him from Denmark. It was solid cast iron and weighed around 240 kilos. On its left side, the halved cross bore some leaf-life round shapes. They alluded to the old crossroads on the banks of the River Cardener.[7] With their circular 'auratisations', they evoked both the crossroads in Manresa and Beuys's Plate Crucifix, which he made at the end of the 1950s and used in the MANRESA action. Nørgaard and Christiansen dragged the heavy Ignatius Halved Cross down the slope to the rocky shore, and lay it there next to a yellow wooden halved cross of the same size, thus letting it appear for a brief moment as a symbol of wholeness.

Station II:
The rocky bank of River Cardener

Nørgaard and his helpers set fire to a rowing boat that had previously been brought to the rocky shore and loaded to capacity with timber. A little further from the water, with the help of a crane, they lifted the bronze halved cross onto a narrow stone staircase built the day before, the Jacob's Ladder, and attached the segment of the cross to its upper end. To the right on the ground lay the other halved cross of painted yellow wood, a heap of salt, twelve loaves of bread, 24 fish and a large metal plate. Nørgaard scattered the salt around using a spade, salted two fish and placed some broken pieces of bread on them. On the shore, the stranded boat that had come from the north burnt brightly, signalling what the artist referred to as a 'cleansing fire'. 'The Inquisition burns; it burns and burns,' as it said later in a text. Christiansen hit the metal plate 27 times with a heavy hammer, leading to the next station.

Station III:
In the middle of the Pont Vell (old bridge)

The two artists set off again. They climbed up the river banks and walked onto the old bridge. From here, a section of the audience had been watching the event so far from there. Bjørn Nørgaard was carrying a white dove in a cage and Henning Christiansen had a pole with a white flag that bore the word peace in Japanese and English. From above, the view looked out onto the remains of the installation on the shore — the salt, fish, loaves, Jacob's Ladder and the two different halves of the cross: the erect Element 1 and the objects lying about, Element 2. Next to it, the boat burning in flames. The scene, with the divided halves of the cross and different materials, was supposed to symbolise waiting for the creative activity of the person who would reassemble them. On the bridge in the middle of the river, Nørgaard let the white dove fly up. Henning Christiansen hammered on the *Friedensblech* (Peace Plate) with a small hammer, then threw it into the River Cardener, an act that commemorated a key phrase from MANRESA:

> Now? Has Element 1 climbed down to Element 2?
> Now? Has Element 2 climbed up to Element 1?
> Where is Element 3?[8]

Station IV:
Cave of Saint Ignatius

The performers and the numerous people watching climbed up the other bank of the river to the Santa Cova. Here, under a rocky outcrop that opens out onto the valley, Ignatius once received his most significant inspirations. Later, a small chapel was built on the spot. Now several elements were gathered on this site in the same way as Bjørn Nørgaard had used them in MANRESA, including a pile of soap, a zinc tub, several bags of plaster, two shoeboxes and electric light bulbs.[9] When he arrived at the spot, Nørgaard repeated the ritual from that action: he walked over bottles, trampled light bulbs, stamped on chunks of plaster, hopped on the floor, rubbed his feet with soap, splashed in the water of the zinc tub, filled two shoeboxes with damp plaster, put his feet in, waited for a short time, stood up and walked laboriously into the neighbouring chapel. One block of plaster broke off, and with the other, he hobbled into the church — a symbolic act that alluded to Ignatius's leg that was shattered by a cannonball.[10] Meanwhile, inside the church, Henning Christiansen performed his percussion piece for hammer and brass plate: *The Peaceful Hammer*, a composition in three movements, prefaced by *The Stupid Hammer* and *The Clever Hammer*.

Station V:
The altar room of the neighbouring Saint Ignatius church
In the crowded church, Bjørn Nørgaard made a bed of damp terracotta blocks, laid out a path to Manresa with traces of plaster and depicted the gathering of the twelve apostles using gravel, upright glass panes and raw eggs cracked on top. In the meantime, Christiansen's 30-minute composition *Der Verwundete – Der Reisende* (The Injured – The Traveller) was played from a tape recorder, which repeated his sound columns from MANRESA. Meanwhile, Nørgaard lay down on the bed like a wounded wanderer. Then the music changed: for another 30 minutes, the bell composition was played by Christophe Charles using sampler and delay techniques. I performed in an Australian shepherd's coat with a dog on a lead. I stood next to the wounded man lying on the bed and remained there motionless for a long time, like a shepherd and guard. Henning Christiansen came in and wrapped the wounded man in gauze bandages as a therapeutic act. Then hammer blows and bells rang out.

Station VI:
In the fireplace room in the Centre for Spirituality
The action arrived at its penultimate destination, the large fireplace room in the adjacent house of spiritual retreat. Once again, Bjørn Nørgaard handed out small fried fish and pieces of bread to those present. I gave a 15-minute lecture on the relationship between Ignatius of Loyola and Joseph Beuys. Henning Christiansen mixed rhythmic interjections and noises into a sound sequence. In doing so, he repeatedly distorted the lecture with musical and poetic elements. Christophe Charles improvised, linking these antagonistic elements together to form a musical unity to conclude the action. The participants then went on a pilgrimage to the end of the action: the opening of the exhibition *Manresa Hauptbahnhof* in the large hall of the Plana de l'Om in the centre of the city.

Station VII: The *Manresa Hauptbahnhof* exhibition in the city of Manresa

At the Plana de l'Om culture and exhibition centre, the curator of the exhibition, Pilar Parcerisas, presented a carefully compiled presentation of all the available works from MANRESA. To her, Joseph Beuys was an artistic nomad. The artist's self-image along these lines shaped all three actions and the exhibitions: Beuys was a pilgrim and traveller, setting off in the spiritual footsteps of Ignatius of Loyola. What carried him is expressed in his much-quoted phrase: 'The mysteries take place in the main station.' Pilar Parcerisas retrospectively clarified these poetic thoughts in the following way: 'If the agility of the soul in Beuys's work is embodied by the symbol of the bird, as it was in ancient Egypt, then the human as an artist on the old bridge across the River Cardener could spread its wings and cry out along with Beuys: "I am flying to you too, MANRESA"'[11].

The exhibition was a combination of drawings and 'scores', i.e. representations and explanations of how the action was carried out, and photographs, catalogues and original objects related to the MANRESA action. Besides, it featured *Manresa '91* scores by Henning Christiansen. Today they have been dispersed among many different museums and collections. Nevertheless, 21 of the original 36 drawings were presented at the exhibition. Harald Szeemann, the great Beuys expert, framed his opening speech around the following question: 'Where is *Element 3*?' To find answers, he drew on Beuys's overall approach to art and the context of his Fluxus phase.

MANRESA as a *Braunraum* (Brown Space)

The colour brown dominates the beautiful valley of Manresa. Especially in the rain, the river water and the porous, moist sandstone take on a rich brown hue. Beuys saw in this colour a sign of the earth, of matter in the process of becoming as well as passing away. In his group works known as *Braunkreuze* (Brown Crosses), he uses this colour tone in its entire range, from simple crosses used for marking to the cross as a symbol imbued with meaning. *Braunkreuz* (Brown Cross) contains the spirit of Fluxus — the movement that overruled any creative rigidity and inventively released itself from the restraints of all hierarchies and iconographies, both artistic and religious. *Braunraum* (Brown Environment) symbolised a *Gegenraum* (counter space) or *Überraum* (supra space) that lay beyond historical space and time in the Beuysian sense of spiritual reality. In Beuys's actions, as Element 2, *Braunraum Manresa* (Brown Space Manresa) represented the symbolisation of powers and the inspirations of the south.

Significantly, Beuys had another brown environment, closely linked to MANRESA: the *Braunraum* Thorvaldsen Museum (Brown Environment of the Thorvaldsen Museum). He understood it as a counter space of art. Beuys loved the Thorvaldsen Museum in Copenhagen and the art of the eponymous Danish artist (1770–1844), who in his biography had overcome the North-South cultural divide in Europe and spent many years of his life in Rome. Thorvaldsen knew how to integrate the concept of beauty into formal rigour, and the ancient ideal of form into cool surface. Beuys saw this ability as an intermediary between the contrasts of North and South. For him, the Thorvaldsen Museum was a presentation of early 19th-century art and of the south comprising ancient, Egyptian, Etruscan, Greek and Roman artworks. So it was already marked by an orientation towards and connection with the South. The *Braunraum* Thorvaldsen Museum also placed an emphasis on Denmark. The two Danish artists, Henning Christiansen and Bjørn Nørgaard brought Element 1 into play in the MANRESA action as a symbolic consolidation of the Nordic counterpart to all things southern. Element 1 and Element 2 stand in contrast to each other here, like modernity and Renaissance, Protestant and Catholic, North and South, and Scandinavia and Rome, as is shown in the score, which was drawn for the action.[12] The *Braunraum* Thorvaldsen Museum is the dialectical counterpart to the Brown Environment Manresa. They both stand for the expansion of the vertical and horizontal axes, for the opening of the transcendental perspective between bottom and top, in the process of ascending and descending and for cultural exchange between East and West, North and South. In between, the artistic person lives and works as a mediator, reminder and activator — as Element 3.[13]

Ignatius transferred mysticism and politics, intuition and rationality, contemplative internal reflection and energetic action onto the militancy of his *Spiritual Exercises* and order; for Beuys, this was continued as a model of disciplined action. But: 'Everything militant must be carried out towards the human being himself,' as Beuys formulated in a discussion with me. 'It must become an inner war, [...] a struggle to attain this consciousness. And that cannot be achieved without discipline or militancy.'[14] These words express the tension between fascination and distance that characterises Beuys's relationship with Ignatius. 'In the quest for new resources of knowledge, spirituality, inspiration, intuition and emotion' — as the Cologne art author Johannes Röhrig sums up Beuys's and Ignatius's points of contact in the catalogue of *Manresa* (1991) — 'people have to move'.[15] Both associate the 'beautiful valley of Manresa'[16] with the idea of terra sancta, psychologically as well as topographically.

Bjørn Nørgaard's cast-iron halved cross summed it up as an image: the verticals of the crossroads and the horizontals of the river as well as the paths on the river shore. In seismographic confusion, the 'Compass from Manresa'[17], in Beuys's later installation *Blitzschlag mit Lichtschein auf Hirsch* (Lightning with Stag in its Glare, 1958–1985), shows no direction over the magnetically and spiritually charged southern earth. From then on, artistic wanderers and religious pilgrims, beginning with Ignatius and Beuys, had to go on their own explorations and make intuitive guesses to locate them using fine distinctions. What united them was their determined and confident search. But there was also something that divided them. Beuys undoubtedly appreciated Ignatius, but he also wanted to overcome ecclesiastical ties. Beuys wanted to transform his thinking to suit everyone and their potential for liberation. This is where their opinions diverged. For the time being?[18]

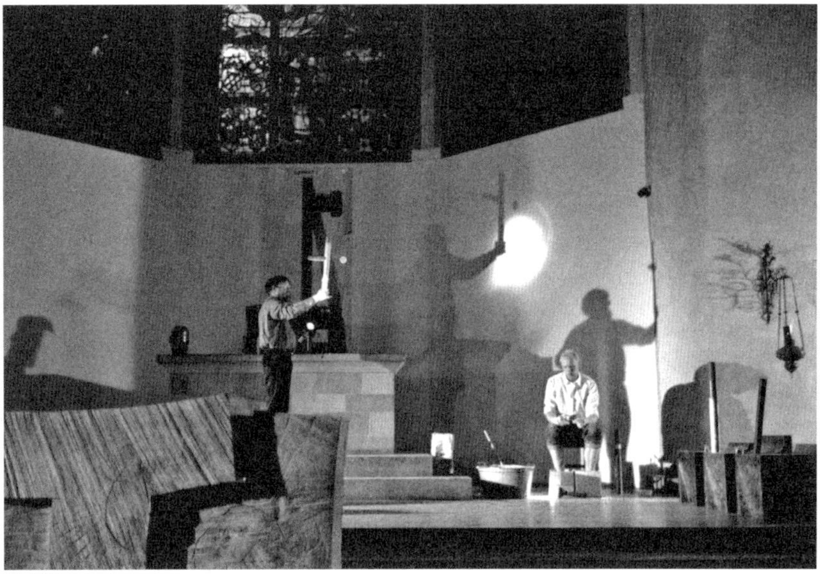

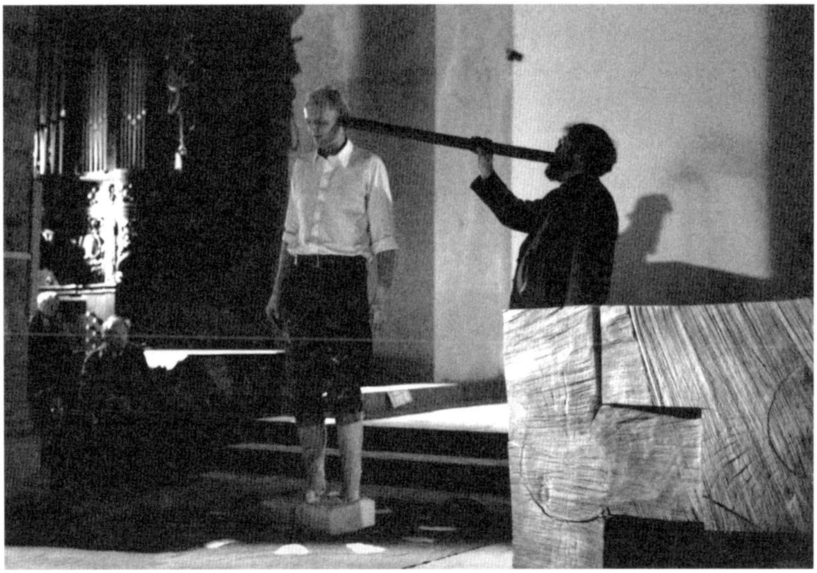

A *Manresa '91* action, Kunst-Station Sankt Peter, Cologne, 21 February 1991.

1
The MANRESA Fluxus demonstration and its commemorative re-enactments have been documented. The action itself was described in Friedhelm Mennekes, *Joseph Beuys. MANRESA: Eine Aktion als geistliche Übung nach Ignatius von Loyola* (Joseph Beuys – Manresa. An Action as a Spiritual Exercise on Ignatius von Loyola), Frankfurt am Main and Leipzig: Insel Verlag, 1992; the commemorative re-enactment by Henning Christian and Bjørn Nørgaard in Cologne 1991 is described in Johannes Röhrig (ed.), *Beuys Manresa. Zeichnungen, Fotos und Materialien zu einer Fluxus-Demonstration*, (Beuys Manresa. Drawings, Photos and Materials for a Fluxus demonstration), Cologne: Kunst-Station Sankt Peter, 1991 [Exh. cat.]; the commemoration of the action in Manresa 1994 is described in Pilar Parcerisas (ed.), *Manresa Hauptbahnhof*, Manresa and Barcelona: Generalitat de Catalunya and Fundació Caixa Manresa, 1994 [Exh. cat.].

2
Röhrig (ed.), *Beuys Manresa*.

3
Mennekes, *Joseph Beuys. MANRESA*.

4
The following details are based on transcripts by Bjørn Nørgaard and recollections of the participants.

5
Röhrig (ed.), *Beuys Manresa*.

6
Pilar Parcerisas (ed.), *Joseph Beuys. MANRESA: A Spiritual Geography*, Barcelona: Tenov Books, 2021, p. 138. In a Beuys's drawing it says: 'Auch zu dir fliege ich, MANRESA', Ibid., p. 14.

7
Illustrations and descriptions in Parcerisas (ed.), *Manresa Hauptbahnhof*, *op. cit.*, pp. 144–147.

8
Mennekes, *Joseph Beuys. MANRESA*, p. 98.

9
Listed ibid. p. 101 ff.

10
Saint Ignatius of Loyola, *A Pilgrim's Journey: The Autobiography of Ignatius of Loyola*, Joseph N. Tylenda, S.J. (trans.), San Francisco: Ignatius Press, 2001. Section 1 and Mennekes, *Joseph Beuys. MANRESA*, pp. 25–27.

11
Parcerisas (ed.), *Joseph Beuys. MANRESA*, p. 158.

12
Illustrated in Parcerisas (ed.), *Manresa Hauptbahnhof*, p. 104.

13
Mennekes, *Joseph Beuys. MANRESA*, pp. 116–123.

14
Friedhelm Mennekes, *Joseph Beuys. Christus DENKEN: THINKING Christ*, Stuttgart: Katholisches Bibelwerk, 1996, p. 37.

15
Röhrig (ed.), *Beuys Manresa*, pp. 30–32.

16
Joseph Beuys's drawing in Mennekes, *Joseph Beuys. MANRESA*, p. 87 and Parcerisas (ed.), *Manresa Hauptbahnhof*, p. 101.

17
According to Beuys, 'Boothia Felix' is a 'small, self-contained cosmos' (quoted in Heiner Bastian, in *Joseph Beuys: Blitzschlag mit Lichtschein auf Hirsch, 1958–1985*, Bern: Benteli, 1986, p. 18). The earth from the plant box which Beuys had 'saved' contained the roots of a plant which he had dug out in 1964 in Manresa; a place that resonated with the symbolic, spiritual and mystical elements in Beuys's work.

18
See the end of the discussion with Joseph Beuys in Mennekes, *Joseph Beuys. Christus DENKEN*, pp. 77, 79.

PETER VAN DER MEIJDEN

MANRESA MULTIPLIED BY TWO / REALITY MULTIPLIED BY THREE: HENNING CHRISTIANSEN, BJØRN NØRGAARD AND JOSEPH BEUYS'S MANRESA

We have become accustomed to viewing Manresa from an elevated perspective, where it appears as a Beuysian reworking of the story of a warrior turned saint, the search for an Element 3 that is the result of a fusion of Western rationalism and Eastern spiritualism, a tableau replete with Christian symbolism. But how would an average visitor have experienced the event? What would it have been like to have been there, that cold winter evening in December 1966 at Galerie Schmela in Düsseldorf?

For one thing, most visitors would have seen the action from the side, through the window. Only a few would have been able to squeeze in through the door into the narrow gallery space itself. Those at the window would have seen a man in a beard, working at a row of tape recorders; behind him was a younger man with long hair who worked various everyday materials with his feet; and furthest back there was an older man wearing a hat, perhaps manipulating an electric apparatus, perhaps holding up a plate with a Christ figure on it, perhaps shooting blobs of margarine at the wall with a bicycle pump. The lucky few inside the gallery space would have seen the man with the tape recorders and the man working with his feet — Henning Christiansen and Bjørn Nørgaard — first, and only after that, on the other side of the chimney in the middle of the back wall and most recognisable of all, Joseph Beuys. Those who managed to squeeze inside would also have been much more conscious of the soundscape, which connected the activities that went on.

Accepting that the whole event took place in a Beuysian atmosphere means expecting the audience to re-read it backwards after seeing Beuys. Would it not be fairer to assume that most visitors would have started to formulate their opinion directly upon entering, developing the story from there? This article discusses MANRESA and *Manresa Hbf* at the meeting point of three oeuvres and as paths that crossed twice, with a 25-year interval. From this point of view, no oeuvre is more important than the others, although the latter event does take the shape of a kind of homage. What this article focuses on is the form these two meetings of oeuvres took and the way that form co-produced the content of the actions.

More specifically, this article treats Henning Christiansen's and Bjørn Nørgaard's ventures into Beuys's conceptual and formal world as, to use an expression used by the former in an article called 'Reality Multiplied by Three', 'neither incorrect nor unimportant', roughly translated.[1] The two artists' contributions are not discussed in Beuysian terms but on their own, and the conclusion is that the two meetings push all three to the edge of their comfort zones. MANRESA brought pervasive sound to Beuys's actions and symbolism to Christiansen's and Nørgaard's otherwise formally-oriented worlds. *Manresa Hbf* presented the latter two with an opportunity to work through their respective understandings of Beuys's artistic project and the spiritual tradition surrounding the city of Manresa, the person of Ignatius of Loyola and the Christian faith in general, while casting new light on the Beuys legacy in the process.

The article is constructed more or less chronologically. It consists of four parts: 'to MANRESA' (1963–1966), 'MANRESA' (1966), 'to *Manresa Hbf*' (1967–1994) and '*Manresa Hbf*' (1994). For the sake of clarity (and brevity), the period from 1994 to the present is not discussed, although Christiansen and Nørgaard continued their dialogue with Beuys and the methods and themes from MANRESA. The narrative is restricted to the elements of Christiansen's and Nørgaard's work that went into MANRESA, the elements of MANRESA that they took with them in their work of the intervening period and the ways in which their understanding of MANRESA and Beuys's oeuvre informed the form and content of *Manresa Hbf*. The procedure does not offer any 'truths' about the central works, only angles;[2] what it does offer is the possibility of multiple understandings of, or multiple takes on, a core of meanings surrounding notions of transformation, enlightenment, responsibility and social change. This will be the highlighted at the end of the article by means of Christiansen's 'Reality Multiplied by Three', which discusses Beuys's use of materials, procedures, tradition and action in the light of his programme to create a third position alongside the conceptual and the experiential realm, a position reaching out to both while not being reducible to either.

To MANRESA, 1963–1966

A couple of words about generational and artistic affiliation to start with. Christiansen met Beuys via Fluxus; Nørgaard met him via a Danish group called Eks-skolen (the Experimental School of Painting, or Ex-School). This may seem unimportant, but it makes a difference, as does the age difference. Christiansen was born in 1932, which made him fifteen years older than Nørgaard, but eleven years younger than Beuys. Nørgaard is a baby boomer and a natural part of the youth revolt against the generation that Beuys belonged to; Christiansen, and the other artists who were somehow involved with Fluxus during the first half of the 1960s, fell exactly in between. Artistically speaking, too, they built a bridge between the two generations, extending well-established artistic traditions into the undefined territory in between art forms, creating hybrids and entirely new forms, characterised (amongst other things) by liveness. Visual artists expanded upon Abstract Expressionism and Tachism to create happenings and events; composers coupled the procedures of Serialism with John Cage's chance operations and embrace of everything that went on in the time frame of the work to create action music; poets took the Beat systems of random text generation and practices such as concrete and sound poetry to give their works a live element. Nørgaard's generation incorporated their artistic revolution in its recipes for a social revolution, whether driven by Provos, hippies or other socio-political rebels.

The connection between early Fluxus and the youth revolt of 1968 was convoluted and indirect, but half a generation on, the Ex-School became deeply involved in it.

Christiansen, a composer, had become aware of Fluxus thanks to DUT (Det Unge Tonekunstnerselskab, the Danish Society for Young Composers), which was instrumental in the organisation of a Fluxus festival in Copenhagen in November 1962. Although not actively involved in the organisational side of things, Christiansen, as a board member, was close to the event. As a result, he ended up participating in several Fluxus events in Denmark and organising a Fluxus-inspired happening of his own at his farm in Kirke Hyllinge, some 50 km east of Copenhagen, in the summer of 1964. Characteristic of his work in this period is the creation of social situations that can be understood as (intellectual) activity without being linkable to any existing form. They tend to focus on everyday actions and to take place amongst the audience.

The first time he met Beuys was during the *Festival der neuen Kunst*, the Festival of the New Art, at Aachen Polytechnic, on 20 July 1964. At this point, their styles were worlds apart: while Beuys contributed with a large-scale action in the auditorium, Christiansen performed small events inside and outside on the campus grounds. When they met again a couple of weeks later, during a festival in Copenhagen called New Concert Phenomena, Happenings, Action Music, in late August / early September 1964, their contributions were equally different: Beuys lay in a roll of felt for eight hours while communicating with the outside world by means of guttural noises (*Der Chef/The Chief*), while Christiansen stirred cups of coffee at timed intervals and presented the resulting brew to members of the audience (*Coffee Pieces*, Op. 24). Beuys had already begun to create complex pieces with symbolic and ritual undertones, while Christiansen composed sparse instruction pieces which hardly required any skill and only made use of the simplest of means.

However, during the summer of 1964, Christiansen decided it was time to move on. He had affiliated himself with the Ex-School, founded in 1961 by painter Poul Gernes and art historian Troels Andersen as an alternative to the art academy. By 1964, it functioned as an artists' group and a happening collective rather than as a school. The group had developed its own brand of minimalism, fuelled by Andersen's knowledge of the Russian avant-garde of the (pre-) revolutionary years (Constructivism, Malevich's *Black Square*) and by works on logical positivism, cybernetics and game theory. On the basis of notions such as Ludwig Wittgenstein's 'elementary propositions' and Rudolf Carnap's 'elementary experiences', the group developed procedures that stressed the constructed nature and object character of their work and downplayed the elevated status of art and the artist. This intellectual atmosphere encouraged Christiansen to develop what became known as 'the new simplicity' in music. When he presented his *Perceptive Constructions*, Op. 28, at the Thorvaldsen Museum in Copenhagen, in October 1965, the work caused a stir. It treated sound as if it was matter, sculpting it in massive columns of sound, separated by silences. Hans-Jørgen Nielsen, an author near to the Ex-School, described them as 'de-dramatised forms' and 'forms without an inner centre'[3], and Christiansen himself insisted that they constituted a new formal alphabet, no longer ruled by the artist's ego.

Nørgaard, too, came to call the forms he developed during his time with the Ex-School 'alphabets'; *sculptural* alphabets to be precise, because he chose to identify himself primarily as a sculptor, even though many of the artists associated with the group moved away from such labels and worked to create works that could no longer be called 'sculpture' or 'painting' but only 'art' and 'object'. His earliest works were semi-figurative, but in a move characteristic of the avant-garde of the time (and of the Ex-School in particular), he embraced basic forms and developed them into action. Among the procedures he experimented with were pouring liquid plaster into cardboard containers and/or through wire mesh barriers ('pourings') and combining everyday objects into impromptu constellations without a base or specific orientation ('concretions'). He created his work in a grey zone between object and performance. Beuys witnessed him in one of these works during a two-day event called Tilstande (Situations) at the Ex-School's Gallery 101 in Copenhagen on 14–15 October 1966, and was so struck by it that he decided to invite Nørgaard to participate in MANRESA, in December of that year.

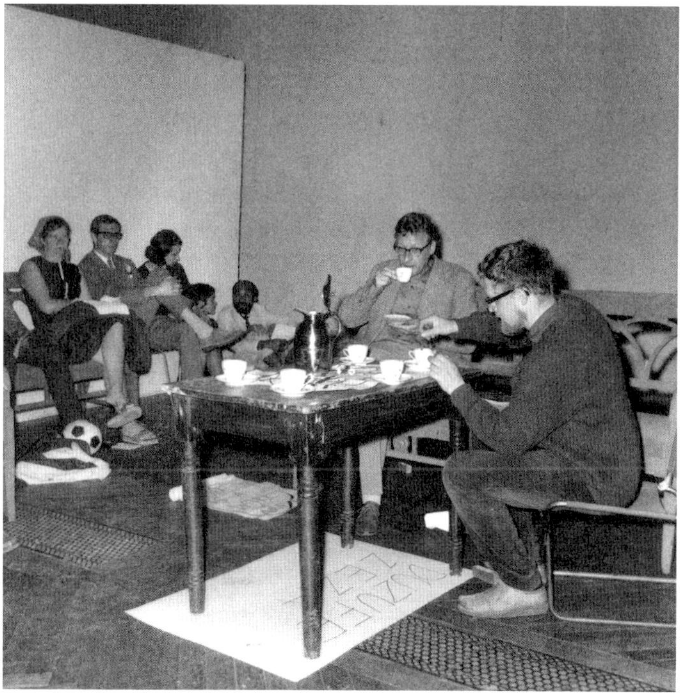

A Henning Christiansen performing one of his *Coffee Pieces*, festival New Concert Phenomena, Happenings, Action Music, Charlottenborg, Copenhagen, 4 September 1964.

The work that struck Beuys was what Nørgaard himself called a 'material action'. During the action, he manipulated various base materials with his feet and ended up casting his feet in plaster. Among the works performed by Christiansen were the *Coffee Pieces*. On 20 November 1966, Beuys wrote a letter to Christiansen, asking him to find out whether Nørgaard would be willing to repeat his action at Galerie Schmela, and inviting Christiansen himself to come and perform his *Coffee Pieces* outside the gallery while he and Nørgaard performed inside. The passage about Nørgaard is especially significant:

> 'Could you find out if it is possible for me to have the young man who did the piece with the feet at Kongensgate?
> Conditions:
> 1. He must repeat the same thing as in Kongensgate
> 2. He must wear the same suit as in Kongensgate, same shoes, etc.
> 3. He must bring the same piece of tape that was played very loudly on the first night.'[4]

Beuys wanted the same person to do the same things, wearing the same clothes to the accompaniment of the same tape; it sounds as if he needed him as a formal element in what was to become MANRESA. The result of the letter was that Christiansen and Nørgaard boarded the former's car in mid-December 1966 to drive to Düsseldorf.

MANRESA, 15 December 1966

Much has been written about MANRESA. The aim here is not to add new information or insights to the material already available, but only to highlight the way it was structured. First, however, it is important to take a closer look at the forms of collaboration that the three artists were acquainted with at this point in time. The Fluxus Festival in Copenhagen in November 1962 that Christiansen witnessed, took the form of often — but far from always — short instruction-based pieces, ascribed to an author but performed by others and performed one after another. The locally-programmed Fluxus events from 1963–1964 he participated in were less strictly organised; pieces could be performed simultaneously and the divide between stage and auditorium was not rigidly maintained.

The forms of collaboration that the Ex-School practiced were equally diverse. Its earliest happenings were semi-improvised and often collective or simultaneous, but as the members' focus on basic forms and elementary procedures grew, they became more schematic, closer to the early Fluxus performances. In contrast to the latter, however, the participants were recognisable by characteristic procedures and/or colours; Nørgaard, for example, often worked with the colours yellow and blue. The event where Nørgaard met Beuys, Tilstande, was organised in partially overlapping time slots, identified by the name of the artist, who was the performer as well. Works were presented in separate rooms, so the artists did not interact. That is also why Beuys did not witness Nørgaard's performance in its entirety: by the time he had finished his own performance, the latter had already started.

The first Fluxus festival Beuys participated in, at the art academy in Düsseldorf in February 1963, was organised along more or less the same lines as the one in Copenhagen, three months earlier. Pieces were presented one after the other and often performed by others than the author him/herself, but he had experienced other formats as well. During *24 Stunden* (24 Hours), at Galerie Parnass in Wuppertal on 5 June 1965, for example, the participants performed simultaneously from 12 midnight until 12 midnight, each in their own room. Likewise, during New Concert Phenomena, Happenings, Action Music in Copenhagen, in the summer of 1964, the artists had for the most part performed separately and under their own names; the only exception is one evening of simultaneous performances which Beuys did not participate in. Most of his actions up until MANRESA had been solo performances. His iconic *How to Explain Pictures to a Dead Hare*, for example, at Galerie Schmela on 26 November 1965, took the shape of a private tour of his own show with a dead hare as the only participant, which the audience could only witness through the window.

Beuys's letter to Christiansen might give the impression that MANRESA was preconceived and pre-planned, and that the two Danish artists' contributions took place within an overall scheme that they had no influence on. That may well have been the intention, but things turned out differently. To begin with, Christiansen was not relegated to the street, as Beuys initially wrote, but was assigned a zone of the gallery space itself. Secondly, the division of the space in three zones meant that the three artists worked side by side and that their actions could freely mix. Finally, Christiansen did not perform his *Coffee Pieces*, but brought a selection of tape works which he played simultaneously, creating a slowly fluctuating soundscape that organised the work temporally in way closely related to the sound 'columns' in *Perceptive Constructions*. The upshot of this is that while Beuys had devised a structure for the piece beforehand — which we will get to in a moment — he had also allowed Christiansen to create and impose a structure of his own.

Thematically, MANRESA drew on the complex of meanings that powered Beuys's *Siberian Symphonies* (no. 1, 1963, and no. 34, 1966). During the first, a Siberian landscape was built on top of a grand piano and metaphorically brought to life by means of a wire, attached to the heart of a hare. In no. 34, which he performed during 'Situations', a dead hare was made to walk from West to East and back West again. The journey from West to East and from the grand piano to the tundra returns in Manresa in the shape of a back-and-forth between the poles of the spiritual to the rational. Life, death and resurrection were rendered present by means of electric sparks off a Geissler tube and a figure of Christ on a round plate. East and West, the spiritual and the rational, were represented by means of two 'stations' in Beuys's section of the room, one centred on a felt half-cross which he completed with chalk at the start of the action, and the other on a box of electronic equipment, including the abovementioned Geissler tube. A third element, simply identified as Element 3, was introduced by means of a sound recording that was played at intervals, together with Christiansen's sound material.

Beuys's tape is a useful key to the action, so it is worth taking a closer look at it. It starts with Beuys's voice:

> Now?[5] Has Element 2 climbed up to Element 1?
> Now? Has Element 1 climbed down to Element 2?

n is the intersection of three transmitting lines
one sculpture
two potential arithmetic
or one and two integrated
and Element 3
—
Fat corner / Fat corner
Filter fat corner
Felt corner
—
BROWN SPACES

After a pause, a female voice asks, 'Good morning, where are you going?', and Beuys answers, 'Thorvaldsen Museum.' After another pause, the first part is repeated, and the recording ends with a variation over the second part to which the lines 'this is FLUXUS speaking' and 'I am flying to you too, MANRESA' are added.

The fat and felt corners were physically present in the room. As with all of Beuys's works, they carry many layers of meaning, but amongst other things they express the ability of art to change fixed situations and actions, the principle of energy and the principle of isolation. Beuys's signature reddish brown colour, that the name 'Brown spaces' (in German: *Braunräume*) refers to, connotates both isolation and blood. It metaphorically encases the room, protecting the energy inside from detrimental influences and turning it into a spiritual battery. In this context of the conservation of flow and power, the Thorvaldsen Museum stands for classicism in art.[6] Between the rules of classicist sculpture and the act of sculpting as a way of changing reality, Element 3 stands for energy that begins to flow again: from the spiritual East to the rational West and back, bringing life to a congealed art and a congealed political and mental landscape.

This type of analysis takes Beuys as its starting point and gives precedence to the Beuysian vocabulary and world of thought. However, Christiansen and Nørgaard brought their own vocabularies and thoughts with them as well. What Christiansen brought along in his car were a number of recordings; among them was the already mentioned *Perceptive Constructions*, but also a piece called *Knocking* and a recording of a poem by Nielsen called *ikke/kan* ('not/can'). The score of *Knocking* instructs a performer to tap on all the sides of a musical instrument or another type of hollow object and to drag it around each time a side has been tapped on. *Ikke/kan* is a visual poem:

<table>
<tr><td>ikke</td><td></td><td></td><td></td></tr>
<tr><td>ikke</td><td>kan</td><td></td><td></td></tr>
<tr><td></td><td>kan</td><td>ikke</td><td></td></tr>
<tr><td>ikke</td><td>kan</td><td>ikke</td><td></td></tr>
<tr><td></td><td>kan</td><td>ikke</td><td>ikke</td></tr>
<tr><td></td><td>kan[7]</td><td></td><td></td></tr>
</table>

Seeing it on paper makes it easier to spot what is going on: can and cannot are joined by their double negation ('cannot not'), adding a third element to the simple opposition that tips the balance in favour of the positive. The exploration of a resonating space in *Knocking* and the play of two oppositional elements and a third in *ikke/kan* are eerily close to the Beuysian idea complex, while remaining firmly rooted in Christiansen's oeuvre. The same can be said of the way the pieces were presented, played simultaneously on three tape recorders and in constantly overlapping patterns. Since 1965, Christiansen had used tape recording as a way of freeing music from the score as the embodiment of the composer's vision and the performance as always unique. On tape, a composition can be inserted into any context and combined with any other recording. This, too, was a way of bringing movement to a congealed art form. The layering of tapes, meanwhile, was seen by Christiansen as a way of making music spatial. On several occasions he has described his sonic construction as 'architecture',[8] a structure in the room that serves as a space for Beuys's work to unfold itself in.

Nørgaard, meanwhile 'manipulated a random number of randomly chosen materials and placed them in relation to his legs.'[9] He filled a 15 cm high wooden frame with lightbulbs, covered the bulbs with a piece of cloth and crushed them with his feet. He stamped on a 30 × 30 × 30 cm cube of clay, once again covered with a piece of cloth, until it was reduced to a 'pillow-shaped mass'. He made a wire grid on top of the wooden frame with the lightbulbs and destroyed it by means of rocking and hopping movements. He used his feet to cover a sheet of Masonite with brown soap. He stepped up in a cardboard box while slowly filling it with flour, moving his feet and legs about in the flour all the time. He dissolved a large quantity of brown soap in a tub with his legs. Finally, he cast his feet each in its own block of plaster. The series of actions falls within a work category that Nørgaard called 'demonstrations'. They were not envisaged as something for the visitors to copy, but as a way of confronting them with their own agency. By working with his feet instead of his hands, he underlined the fact that no skill was required and by focusing on the simplest of transformations, he tried to make the viewers aware that everything could be transformed, everywhere and by anyone.

The juxtaposition of these three different attitudes in three freely interacting zones in Galerie Schmela produced a clash of intentions; not one that could not be resolved, but certainly one that pushed all three artists to the edge of their comfort zones. Christiansen and Nørgaard produced work that was intentionally rendered as simple as possible, so they could communicate that they required no special skill to make and no special knowledge to understand. Their works communicated in a metonymical manner, their materials and procedures connected to broader artistic and societal notions by extension. Specifically, they wanted the simplicity of their work to stand in for a broader democratisation of art and, in the end, of society.

Among the things that were purged from their work were metaphor and narrative. Beuys, on the other hand, made frequent use of both. In 1968, Christiansen tried to formulate his understanding of Beuys's way of communicating via his art in the aforementioned 'Reality Multiplied by 3', subtitled 'Four Epistles on Beuys's Working Methods.'[10] In the text, he explained how Beuys used his materials and procedures, artistic traditions and live action to communicate meaning. This may sound abstract, but we will return to the text later for closer inspection. What is important for now is that Beuys, as Christiansen understood him, worked with meaning on many different levels. All three used their materials and procedures as signifiers of some sort, but (at least according to Christiansen) Beuys alone also drew on existing sign systems, narrative oppositions, metaphorical transformations and so on.

This is best illustrated by taking a closer look at the very title of the action, MANRESA. There is not a text about the action that does not mention Ignatius of Loyola, who underwent a spiritual transformation in the city of Manresa and emerged as the founder of the Jesuit order. However, Manresa is a physical location as well. It is a city with a particular layout, situated in a particular landscape. As mentioned, the *Siberian Symphony* series was concerned with geography: a landscape was created on top of the grand piano and a laborious walk was mimed from the East to the West and back again. In the case of MANRESA, it is the title itself that adds the geographical aspect. However, the action not only activates the city's location, but its history as well: how Ignatius came to Manresa as a wounded soldier, how he spent his time there meditating and how he emerged from the city as an enlightened soul. The title renders Manresa present both as a geographical location, as a moment in time, as a place to arrive at and depart from and as a threshold or liminal space where a transformation can take place.

For the story of Christiansen's and Nørgaard's meeting with Beuys's MANRESA in 1966, and with the memory of the action and the real city in 1994, it is important to stress once again that neither of them, at that point in time, was invested in storytelling or history. Both came to embrace them, but, as the next section will show, that took time — not to mention the transformative experience of engaging in real struggle for the transformation of society. In 1966, Christiansen and Nørgaard had banned narration in all its forms from their work in favour of simple materials and procedures. Beuys, on the other hand, created complicated tableaus in which materials and forms both acted as themselves, as metonymies and as metaphors. Inescapably, Beuys's use of stories and history affected Christiansen's and Nørgaard's work within the scope of MANRESA, while their minimalism, at the same time, affected Beuys's actions. Christiansen's ever-changing soundscape gave continuity to Beuys's two-part (or three-part, if one counts Element 3, which was not rendered physically present in the room) structure and Nørgaard's simple progression of actions formed a neutral counterpoint to some of Beuys's more symbolically charged actions, such as the showing of the plate with the figure of Christ or the manipulation of the Geissler tube. Their presence in the room together was not — and could never be — the simple one-after-another of the early Fluxus festivals, the simultaneity of the later festivals and happenings or even the next-to-each-other of three individual performances that took place at the same time. Their works took place next to each other, but in a space they created together, both physically (visually and sonically) and narratively — a space that was not native to any of the three artists, but which nevertheless could encompass all three of their works, if somewhat uncomfortably.

To *Manresa Hauptbahnhof*, 1967–1994

After MANRESA, Christiansen collaborated with Beuys on several other actions: *Hauptstrom* (Galerie Franz Dahlem, Darmstadt, 20 March 1967), *Eurasian Staff* (Galerie Nächst St. Stephan, Vienna, 2 July 1967 and Wide White Space gallery, Antwerp, 9 February 1968), *ö ö Programm* (Art Academy Düsseldorf, 30 November 1967), *I am trying to set (make) you free* (Art Academy Berlin, 27 February 1969), *...or should we change it* (Städtisches Museum Mönchengladbach, 27 March 1969), *Celtic (Kinloch Rannoch) Scottish Symphony* (Edinburgh College of Art, 23–30 August 1970) and *Celtic +~~~* (Basel, 5 April 1971). He spent long periods in Düsseldorf [11] and saw Beuys often. Their proximity changed the way they worked. Christiansen said about *Hauptstrom*: 'Actually, Beuys and I have never agreed upon any details. He simply showed trust. I built up and tried to follow him and my own ideas.' [12] The actions were the result of an exchange between the two, both before and during the performance.

Christiansen's contributions vary considerably, from multiple to single tape works, from composed music to improvisation and from appearances side-by-side with Beuys to active involvement in the action. His work with Beuys draws upon his own work as a composer but places it in a new light. *Eurasian Staff, 82min Fluxorum Organum Op. 39*, for example, a work for organ which he composed especially

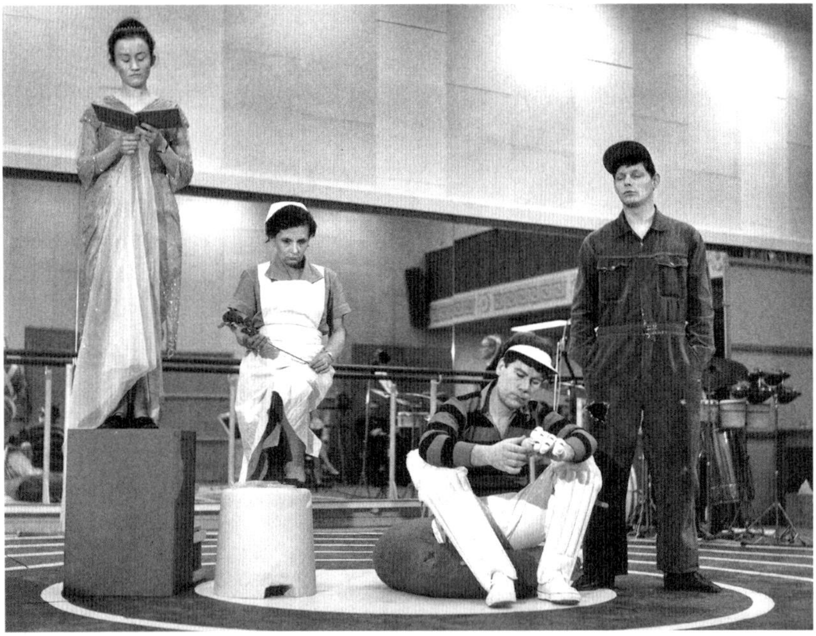

B Henning Christiansen, *Nice weather today, isn't it, Ibsen?*, Op. 37, 1966. Performance at Odd Fellow Palæet, Copenhagen, 19 April 1968. Set design: Bjørn Nørgaard.

for the action *Eurasian Staff*, is related to his work with architectural music via its clarity of structure, but also to his experiments with taped compositions that make it possible to insert the work into a context of the composer's own choosing. The piece follows Beuys's manipulation of the heavy copper staff from *Eurasian Staff*, the notes rising as he raises it up to the four points of the compass and so on, freeing the music from the organ at the Liebfraukirche in Düsseldorf because it was taped. However, as with MANRESA, the title *Eurasian Staff*, paired with Beuys's actions, gives it a meaning beyond these rather abstract considerations surrounding the nature of music and the importance of context.

The back-and-forth between form and meaning in *Eurasian Staff* makes a stunning contrast to one of Christiansen's main works from the mid to late sixties, *Nice weather today, isn't it, Ibsen?* (originally, *Dejligt vejr i dag, n'est-ce pas, Ibsen?*), Op. 37, written in 1966 and premiered in 1968. For want of a better word, the work is an opera. It is certainly a combination of music (by Christiansen), text (a libretto by Nielsen) and visuals (stage design by Nørgaard). However, there is no story or theme. The opera is extremely rigidly organised. The audience does not sit in front of the stage, but around four concentric circles on the floor. The four singers, a soprano, an alto, a tenor and a bass, are each assigned to their own ring. They are recognisable by their clothes, by an attribute and by the way they move. The soprano wears a dress, holds a handkerchief and has a red wooden box as her attribute; the alto is dressed as a nurse, holds a rose and has a white cylinder as her attribute; the tenor wears a cricket outfit, holds a ball and has a green pillow as his attribute; and the bass wears workers' clothes, holds a yoyo and has a plastic cone as his attribute. They always return to a particular pose, the soprano standing, the alto sitting, the tenor reclining and the bass lying down. Both the libretto and the music are circular. The first scene is the same as the fifth, the fourth mirrors the second and the third is the point of balance. As Christiansen writes in his introduction to the score: 'The shapes are sounds, the movements are the time between sounds. Just as the music, the sounds and the text move around in a circle, the singers move through all the forms and back to their original starting point.'[13] In the opera, Christiansen and Nørgaard show what they learned from their Ex-School days and their work with primary forms.

However, more than a culmination point it is a point of transition. What makes it so is the fact that the score not only identifies the piece as a chamber opera, but as a 'ritual' or a 'mass' as well. For Christiansen's part, the double connotation of art and religion is connected with the church organ in *Eurasian Staff, 82min Fluxorum Organum* and with Beuys's use of spirituality. The composition freed the organ from its roots in Christian liturgy but kept the religious connotations. For Nørgaard's part, it has to do with a growing interest in social practices and conventions. After participating in MANRESA, he spent three months with Beuys in Düsseldorf as a visiting artist at the art academy. During his stay he created thirty objects along the lines of those he made at the Ex-School, which he showed during the class's end-of-term exhibition. He concluded his stay with a contribution to the performance series *Deutsch-Dänische Tage* (German-Danish Days), at Galerie Aachen from 15–22 April 1967, engaging with materials in order of density, hardness, consistency and flexibility while standing up, sitting down and lying down.

This systematic and materially oriented way of working, however, was replaced with a more socially oriented one during the latter half of the 1960s. Nørgaard embarked on a series of actions together with his partner, Lene Adler Petersen, that explored the potential of ritual. In his sculptural demonstrations, Nørgaard had regarded context as something extraneous to his alphabets of shapes, but now he came to see it as a material to work with. Instead of simple forms and materials, the two turned their attention to cultural signs in actions that shifted the focus of the work from the manipulation of materials to the inscription of codes and meanings on their own living bodies.

An important group of works revolved around the image of the Female Christ, a recoding of Christ's self-sacrifice as a traditionally female trait. In the movie *The Girl in the Green Dress* (1969), Adler Petersen is seen moving along a red line to a cross on the wall, where she mimes various crucifixion poses. It is difficult not to see references to *Siberian Symphony, Thirty-Fourth Movement. Sentence*, during which Beuys made a hare move along a line from

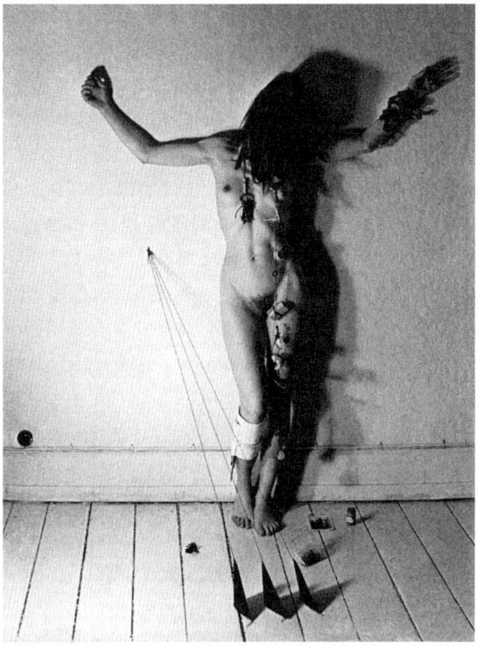

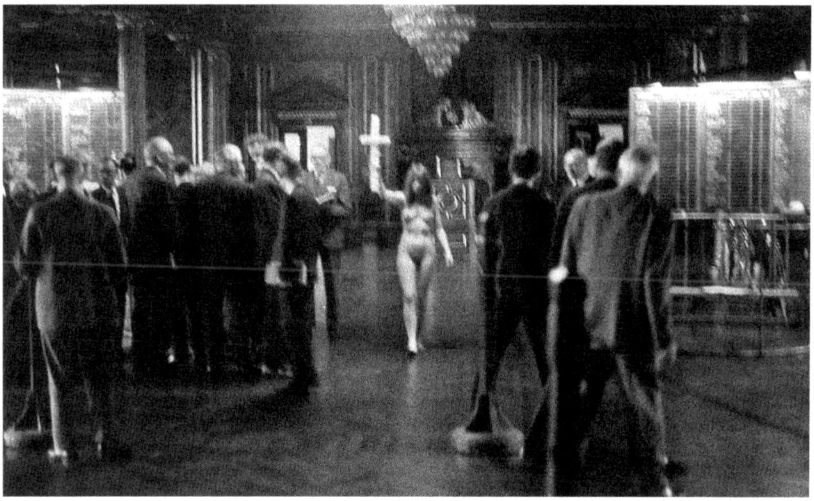

C Film still from the movie *The Girl in the Green Dress*, 1969. Camera: Bjørn Nørgaard. B/W, 8 mm, 9 minutes 4 seconds.

D Lene Adler Petersen and Bjørn Nørgaard, *Expulsion from the Temple/Nude Female Christ I*, Stock Exchange, Copenhagen, 29 May 1969.

West to East and back again, and to MANRESA, where he completed a half-cross. The best-known work of the series, *The Expulsion from the Temple/Nude Female Christ I* (1969), however, was very different in spirit. It consisted of Adler Petersen walking naked through the Copenhagen stock exchange, carrying a cross, as a reference to Christ's cleansing of the temple. Here, the reference is not to Beuys, but to the youth revolt and its rejection of materialism and capitalism. Nørgaard's and Adler Petersen's collaborative work of the late 1960s referred to art as well as to the political climate of the day. It was part-work, part-activism. The point is crucial for an understanding of the different ways in which Nørgaard and Christiansen engaged with Beuys's work and thought.

Christiansen was in Düsseldorf when Beuys founded the *Deutsche Studentenpartei*, the German Students Party, on 22 June 1967. The move was prompted by the shooting of student activist Benno Ohnesorg by the German police during a demonstration against a visit by the Shah of Persia, and as such, it was an explicitly political gesture. However, Beuys also identified the party as Fluxus Zone West, the Western point of a fluctuating movement between East and West, which ties it closely to his own work and especially the idea of the 'social sculpture', meaning art's ability to alter the shape of society. Christiansen was a co-signatory of the founding document and became a party representative in Denmark. On 10 May 1968, he organised a party day at Nikolaj Church in Copenhagen during which his and Nørgaard's approach to art and politics met. Christiansen had tried to invite both Beuys and his student Johannes Stüttgen, who did a lot of work for the party in Germany, but neither could come, so it became a purely Danish affair. During the event, *Eurasian Staff, 82min Fluxorum Organum* was performed live on the church organ. Meanwhile, Nørgaard unrolled a long roll of paper on the floor in the shape of a shepherd's crook and turned it into a 'party landscape' by scattering various materials, objects and items of clothing on it, while Nielsen simultaneously wrote down on the floor all that Nørgaard was doing. Then, Nørgaard made a speech together with the linguist Ole Stig Andersen, co-editor of the countercultural magazine *Hætsjj*, in which it was claimed that new times were coming and that the new era

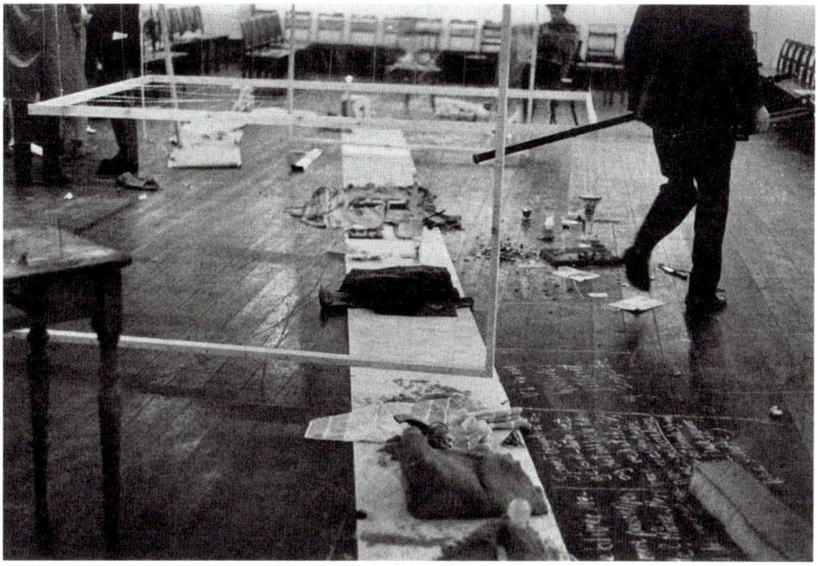

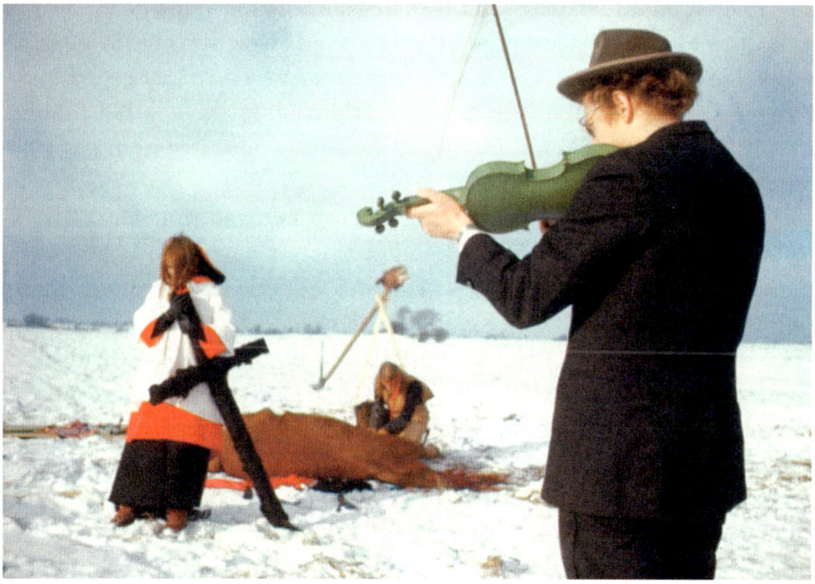

E Bjørn Nørgaard, *Party Landscape*, 10 May 1968. Installation/ action during 'Eurasian Staff (Nordic version)', Nikolaj Church, Copenhagen.

F Bjørn Nørgaard, *Stable/Ritual Dissection of a Horse*, also known as 'The Horse Sacrifice', Kirke Hyllinge, 30 January 1970. From left to right: Lene Adler Petersen (holding a cross), Bjørn Nørgaard (butchering the horse) and Henning Christiansen (playing a green violin).

demanded a new kind of political organisation and a new political language. By implication, the sober actions, the everyday materials and the factual recording of the event became that new language: simple but symbolic and locked in a permanent exchange between East and West, spirit and reason, by means of the *Eurasian Staff*. Beuys's part-symbolic, part-real way of engaging in politics met with Nørgaard's countercultural take on politics in a way that was, once again, not exactly a clash, but not entirely comfortable either.

Nørgaard's and Adler Petersen's work with rituals culminated in a work called *Stable/Ritual Dissection of a Horse* (in Danish, *Stald/Rituel dissektion af en hest*) which was performed during the exhibition Tabernakel, at Louisiana Museum of Modern Art in Humlebæk, just north of Copenhagen, in 1970. The original intention was to stable a horse in one of the rooms of the museum, to look after it and then to butcher it and display its remains in pickle jars. However, the museum wanted nothing to do with horses or butchering, so the horse ended up in a field in Kirke Hyllinge instead, where it was shot and dissected on a cold January day, while Adler Petersen sang a hymn to the dead horse and Christiansen played a green violin. Because the action could not take place in the context of the museum, as was originally intended, Nørgaard and Adler Petersen chose the media as an alternative public space. The action was presented as a protest against the war in Vietnam, but the massive attention it got was not fuelled by anti-war sentiment but by fury at what was considered to be cruel treatment of an animal.

During the same exhibition, Beuys showed the work *Trans-Siberian Railway*. The work itself consists of two empty canvases, their faces turned against the walls, and at some distance from them, two objects identified as *Sendern (2 × Fettfüsse) Holz-Farbe-Wachs* (Transmitters (2 × Fat Feet) Wood-Paint-Wax). During the exhibition, Danish film director Ole John [Povlsen] made a movie of the work. The movie, which lasts for 22 minutes, is mostly static. Apart from a some shaking and doubling, the only thing that happens is that Beuys appears, says 'Gespräch am Strand zu Land' ('Conversation on the beach ashore'), walks up to the canvases, nails them to the wall and draws a line from the canvas to the left to the two transmitters. Beuys himself said about the action: 'acoustically speaking, there are only the hammer blows, but they are not artificial hammer blows but the real hammer blows that were necessary to place the objects in the room. All that happened were that these objects were put into place, the thing was constructed, installed the normal way, and then the film ends.'[14] Next to the sound of the butcher's gun in *Ritual Dissection of a Horse*, the hammer blows seem very quiet indeed. Beuys's minimal action is significant because of its implications, not because of its direct effects. Nørgaard was never able to shake off the name of 'the horse butcher', but Beuys's hammer blows would remain unregarded until Christiansen picked up on them years later.

During the years that followed, action and ritual became life for Nørgaard and Adler Petersen. They engaged in a series of attempts to start new communities. An event called *Dumpingfestival for kulturvarer* (Dumping Festival of Cultural Goods) in a park in Copenhagen, devoted to collective creation, became the start of a series of actions geared towards the establishment of a 'tribe' that turned art into a way of living and acting. The most spectacular of these was the so-called *Livø Action*, during which 18 activists boarded a ship filled with cattle, pigs and seed to plant 200 acres of land in order to start anew on the island of Livø, in a fjord in the north of Jutland. They managed to land, but before they had even ploughed a single furrow, the police showed up sent them away. The ship and the settlers then sailed to the mainland town of Løgstør, where they rented a farm. They had to give up within a year because the effort was not feasible economically, but a later attempt at something similar worked very well. In order to appropriate the means of production, they bought a printing shop in Copenhagen and transformed into the collectively-owned and managed Eks-Skolens Trykkeri, which exists until this very day.

Meanwhile, Christiansen had his own worries. His aim throughout the sixties had been to create work that could be understood by all, but he had been misunderstood time and time again. He had wanted to demystify art and to make it accessible for all, but he was seen as everything but a popular artist. As he wrote in a text dated 7 June 1971: 'That's where the difficulties start, how to avoid looking down on people, to patronise them, to shape one's material so that nobody reacts

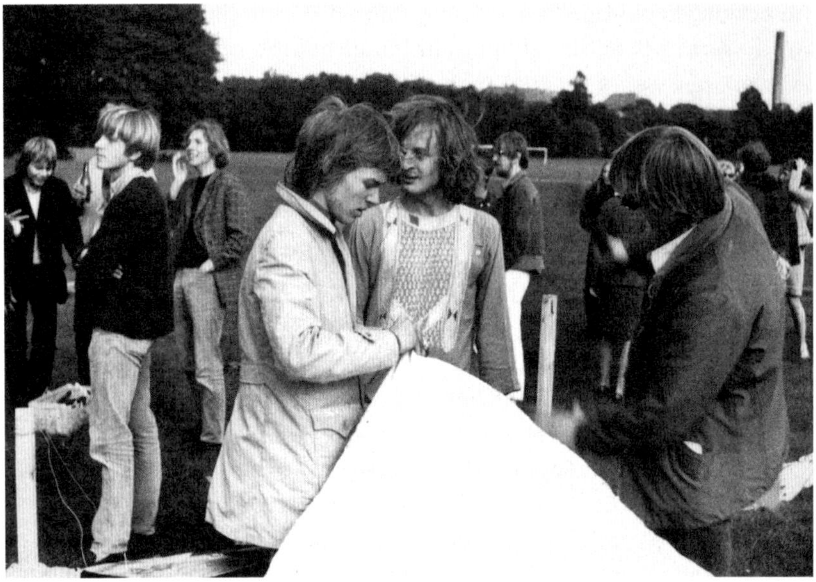

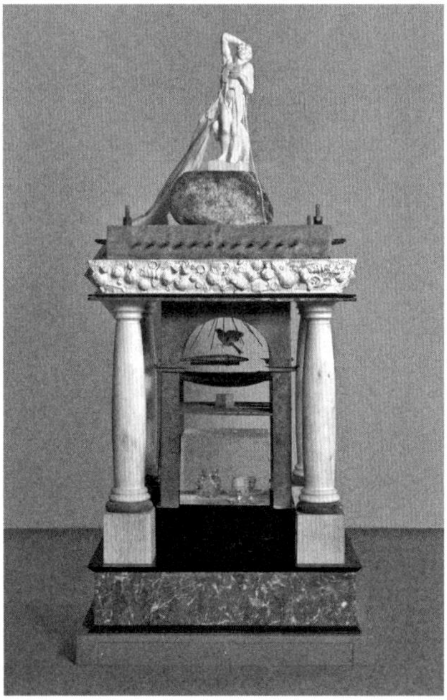

G Dumping Festival of Cultural Goods, Fælledparken, Copenhagen, September 1968. Standing in the middle: Bjørn Nørgaard.

H Bjørn Nørgaard, *Christian III's Mausoleum*, 1975. Marble, concrete, plaster, iron, wood, ceramics, acrylic, fabric, 188 × 83 × 83 cm, ARoS, Aarhus.

because one has made a wrong choice and how does one avoid a commotion about the wrong sides of a work.'[15] Instead of trying to get his political message across by means of radical formal innovations, he decided to focus on radical content. He embraced popular forms such as the waltz but used them to communicate a vision for Denmark — and indeed for the whole of humanity — based on the local community, its double rootedness in landscape and history, solidarity in the face of oppression, collectivism and the rejection of materialism and capitalism. He moved to a farm on the island of Møn, became a member of the Danish Communist Party and actively engaged in the work of its Vordingborg circle, where his main aim was to convince the local farmers of the necessity to take a stand against the political elite. He also wrote music for film and TV and for activist theatre groups such as Skifteholdet (The Work Shift, 1972–1991), which campaigned against Denmark's membership in the EU and for better working conditions and fair pay for the working class.

Nørgaard, too, emerged from his activist period in 1971–1973 with a new focus on community and history. Improbable though it may seem, he began to create monumental sculptures that explicitly referred to the sculptural tradition, while at the same time criticising it. His work *Christian III's Mausoleum* (1975), which is modelled on a monument from the 1570s by the Belgian sculptor Floris of Antwerp, combines marble with concrete and a reproduction of Michelangelo's *Dying Slave*, with a real egg in a real eggcup. The same eclectic choice of materials and images can be seen in what he called his 'tableaux', installations that combined references to the worlds of high art, politics and the everyday, in scenes full of contrasts and clashes. *Marat – who was Corday?*, for example, an assemblage from 1976, is modelled on Jacques-Louis David's famous *Death of Marat* (1793), but where David's Marat only has a pen and paper lying next to him, Nørgaard places him near a table with an egg, a candle, a knife, a loaf of bread, a lightbulb, a diary, a Donald Duck cartoon and the Bible. Together with the question about the person of his murderer, the objects — strongly reminiscent of the objects in his 'party landscape' from 1969 — refer to the everyday motives that power history. These works were still about art and the everyday, but they no longer tried to reconcile the two.

Instead, they sought to generate productive clashes at every possible level, from material to process to content.

From the late 1970s onwards, Nørgaard began to extend his stock of styles and symbols to encompass cultures from across the entire world and from all times. He also engaged in a new collaboration with some of his old comrades (Gernes always used to refer to his Ex-School colleagues as 'comrades') named Arme & Ben, (Arms and Legs). The aim was to create what Nørgaard called a 'popular classicism'. Art had to be transformed from a thin veneer to cover the brutal truths of capitalism to something truly social. Openness and accessibility were the key words. The results were colourful and monumental, and often consisted of many different materials. The members of Arme & Ben embraced narration, made use of easily recognisable images and had no qualms about repeating elements and shapes that worked. It was up to the viewer to decode their meaning.

If Nørgaard moved from action and activism to sculpture, Christiansen's work of the 1980s was characterised by a new stress on the performance itself. Although he had been involved as a performer in several of Beuys's actions, he had always seemed to prefer the role of the composer. His only sallies into the realm of visual art — apart from his visually often very appealing scores — were the occasional multiple or object. With a series of works involving birds, he moved into a hybrid country he was later to explore in a new series of collaborations with Nørgaard, in which installation art meets performance art. To support Beuys in his campaign on behalf of the Green Party in 1980, Christiansen played tapes with birdsong mixed with piano and voice in the tent the party operated from in Düsseldorf. He called it 'anti-consumption music for the Green Party', adding: 'the birds chased the noise of the city from the tent and changed the space of the tent so one felt alive inside.'[16] In 1985, he created a *Symphonia Natura* together with Lorenzo Mammi, making use of animal sounds recorded at Rome Zoo. He exhibited sheep during the 1988 edition of the Ars Electronica festival in Linz, Austria, and in 1992, the Green Party's canaries made a live appearance in an installation at Emily Harvey Gallery in New York. Another invention that drew him into the borderland between installation and performance art was the 'green ear', as 1985 was

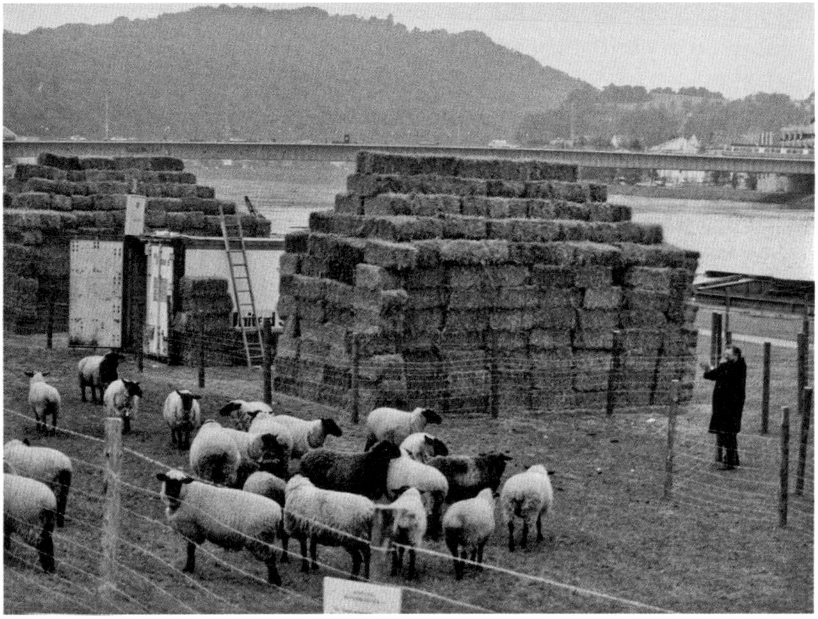

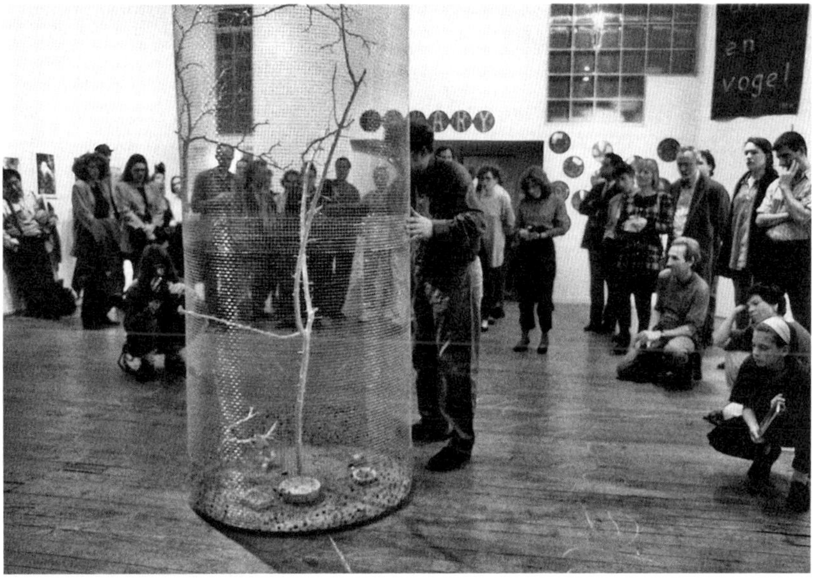

I Henning Christiansen performing *Sheep instead of Violins*, Op. 186, Ars Electronica festival, Linz, 14–17 September 1988.

J Henning Christiansen performing the action *Canary Wisdom, io am en vogel* during the opening of the exhibition *I am a bird/io am en vogel*, Emily Harvey Gallery, New York, 24 April–23 May 1992.

'Green Ear Year': by painting his own and other people's ears green, he created an art without censorship. A third inroad to the world of installation and performance art was the hammer, already mentioned in connection with Beuys's *Trans-Siberia Railway* from 1970: bells and percussion instruments, and very often a hammer applied to metal, created compositions that pounded sense into the listeners' ears and heads by means of sounds rich in overtones and undertones.

In a text from 1986 called 'From Action to Production', Christiansen described the potential he recognised in live action: 'Action is a way to recover the primal... One makes a personal appearance and tries to resolve something primal for oneself and a usually rather small audience of extremely attentive people. There is a salon-like, exclusive, excessive air to it, but it is a ragged salon and a shabby form of exclusivity.'[17] The text marks the start of something new, the new series of collaborations with Nørgaard who for ten years now had worked mainly with sculpture. The first focus of their work together was *Tiefland* (Lowland), a series of actions that fused Christiansen's work with sound at the meeting point of the unruly and the orderly — the animal sounds, the aural freedom of the 'green ear' and the hammer blows — with Nørgaard's new exploration of meaning-making systems and the social nature of understanding.

The first in the series, performed at the Teatro Olimpico in Rome on 9 November 1986, had three titles: *Tiefland – Concerto per telefono – Musica Parallela*. Christiansen's and Nørgaard's part, the *Tiefland* from the title, emerged from a plan for a new Beuys/Christiansen action that never materialised because of Beuys's illness and death in January 1986. It became a memorial performance instead, also featuring American Fluxus artists Philip Corner and Emmett Williams, American conceptual artist Terry Fox and Italian composer Walter Marchetti. Corner, Marchetti and Williams performed simultaneously on stage, Fox played a piano string he had stretched from the edge of the stage to the balcony and Christiansen and Nørgaard performed together with some chickens in the orchestra pit. The pit had been fenced off with chicken wire and was lit up with alternating red, green and blue light. The audience could follow the goings-on inside on a monitor. The mode of their collaboration resembled that of the German Student Party Day, with Christiansen playing some of his works on tape and performing others live, while Nørgaard created a landscape out of clay, plaster, gravel, water, syrup, glass, mirrors and a table. However, they broke off their actions every 20 minutes to climb a high ladder and perform an action as well.[18] These actions were not collaborations between a composer and a visual artist, like *Nice weather today, isn't it, Ibsen?*, or meetings of a composer under a shared theme, like the party day, but meetings of two artists in a performance in several media.

Christiansen and Nørgaard continued their collaborations with further elaborations on the *Tiefland* theme: *Lowland – as it emerges* (Oslo, 1987), *Lowland – sun, moon, landscape* (Copenhagen, 1987), *Lowland – Deep in my Hirsch* [Deer] *Heart* (Malmø, 1988), *Lowland – The Sheep Are Still Standing There, Watching* (Aarhus, 1988) and *Lowland Trilogy – The Sleeping Man, the Throne, the Boat* (Sydney, 1990). In Oslo and Aarhus, the two were assisted, not by chickens, but by sheep. Christiansen described them in a letter to the director of Musikhuset in Aarhus as 'a "biblical" visual feature' and assured him that they would not be slaughtered; they simply had to act natural.[19] It was the memory of Nørgaard's dissected horse that made people nervous, but the sheep were Christiansen's contributions. They were needed for the movements and sounds they made, which were amplified so they could be heard throughout the action.

Reviews of the *Tiefland* series often focus on the visual aspect, but a review of the version in Oslo in *Danish Music Magazine* manages to address the sonic aspect as well. The reviewer starts by describing the layout of the space where the action was to take place. It was fenced off by means of chicken wire, just like the orchestra pit in Rome, and there was a stack of materials (plaster, clay, wood, glass, mirrors, water, stone) and some tools (a hammer, a spade, a broom, a brush), but instead of chickens there were five sheep, amply provided with hay. The orchestra pit/stage situation from Rome had been copied by incorporating a space on the first floor where there was a grand piano, two high ladders and some props (two glass bowls, spoons, a fish, a loaf of bread, bags of flour and salt, water, beer, a water pistol, a rose, a stone, a wooden plank). The performance lasted four hours in total, three times 50 minutes in the downstairs room, interspersed with three times ten minutes and a final 60 minutes on the first floor. During 50-minute sessions in the downstairs room, Nørgaard built a landscape, while Christiansen sat at a desk writing or speaking into a microphone, and a tape with natural sounds (machine sounds, voices, animal sounds) created continuity. The sounds of the sheep and the actions were also amplified and mixed with the sounds on tape. On the wall behind them, images of cities, landscapes, sculptures and so on were projected. In the upstairs room, Christiansen and Nørgaard took each of the objects, carried them up the ladders, showed them to the audience and dropped them again — all but the glass bowls, which they hit arrhythmically with the spoons. The action ended with Christiansen showing what he had written ('BEUYS', 'PIT', and so on) and Nørgaard lying down on a bed of clay, plaster and syrup.

Nearly all of these elements also featured in *Manresa Hbf.* Christiansen wrote and recited, Nørgaard built. The glass bowls were replaced with metal sheets that Christiansen hit with a hammer, but Nørgaard employed many of the same materials: the plaster and the clay, the syrup (for energy), the fish (for Christ), the bread (the Holy Communion) and the salt ('salt of the earth', Christ's disciples). Even the images from the subtitle of the last version of *Tiefland*, the sleeping man, the throne and the boat, were present. The actions had started as a homage to Beuys, and Christiansen and Nørgaard developed the idea further by creating a complex network of actions and symbols that combined Beuys's illness and death with their experience of MANRESA and the cultural and religious connotations of everyday objects and images.

Apart from the *Tiefland* series, *Manresa Hbf* also had a precursor in the action *Manresa '91*, at Friedhelm Mennekes's Kunst-Station Sankt Peter in Cologne, on 21 February 1991. Nørgaard did not participate in person, so strictly speaking the action need not concern us here. However, he was present in spirit and represented by means of his work, the signature plaster feet. The event was organised to mark the opening of the exhibition *Beuys Manresa*. Christiansen played Beuys's MANRESA tape and some of his own pieces from 1966, but mixed them with new works, exactly as he would do three years

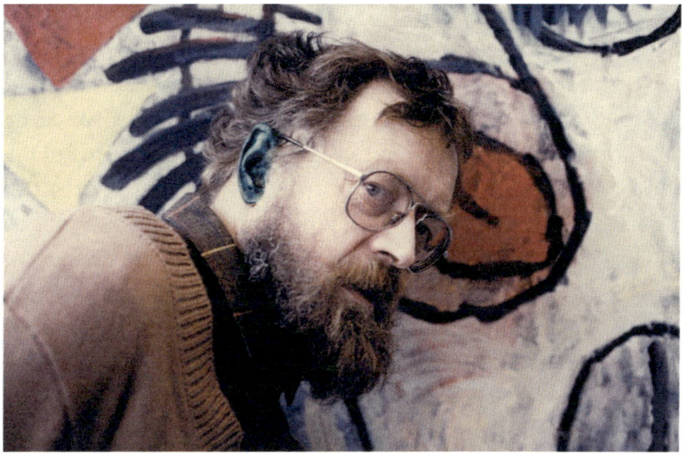

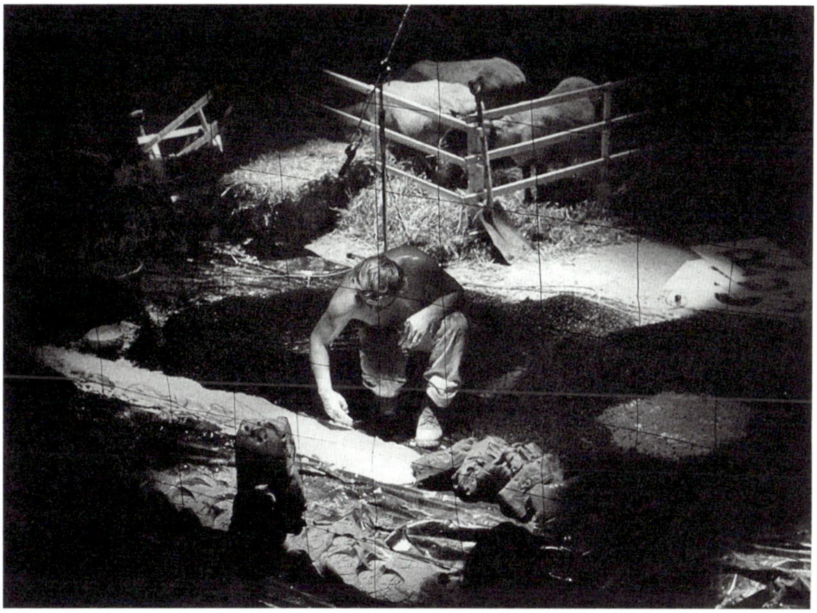

K Henning Christiansen with green ear, photographed at Aarhus Kunstmuseum. Year unknown.

L Bjørn Nørgaard performing during the action *Tiefland–As It Emerges*, Henie Onstad Kunstsenter, Høvikodden, Oslo, 28 March 1987.

later in *Manresa Hbf.* The green ear was incorporated, as was the bird sound that now featured so often in his work. Nielsen's *Ikke/kan* was played while Nørgaard's plaster feet were performed, now under the title 'Schritte' (Steps), and Christiansen himself played on his Stone Age Gramophone, a turntable on which small rocks made a natural clacking and rattling noise. The action was subtitled 'Der Verwundete / Der Reisende' (The Wounded / The Pilgrim), which can refer to Loyola as well as to Beuys. The title is as important in connection with *Manresa Hbf* as the formal elements, as it creates an ambiguous space in which Beuys, Loyola and even Christ (as the wounded one in Beuys's installation *Show Your Wound* (1974–1975) can change places as wanderers and sufferers.

Manresa Hauptbahnhof, 4 November 1994

In 1966, Christiansen and Nørgaard arrived in Düsseldorf armed with their own oeuvre and what they knew about Beuys's work and thought. When they arrived in Manresa in 1994, the situation was more or less the same — apart from the fact, that is, that 28 more years had passed and that they had the experience of *Tiefland* and other collaborative efforts to work with. The two artists no longer occupied their own zone, as they had in the original MANRESA, but worked parallel to one another in a series of scenes or (to adopt the railway terminology of *Manresa Hbf*) stations. There were six of them; not a number that can be related to the fourteen Stations of the Cross, to the life of Ignatius of Loyola or even to his Spiritual Exercises, which are divided into four thematic weeks and designed to be carried out over a period of 28–30 days. They are, however, closely connected to the geography of Manresa. The stations Christiansen and Nørgaard passed on their way were the shrine of La Guia, the bank of the River Cardener, the Old Bridge across the river, the Cave of St. Ignatius, the Baroque church next to the cave and the meeting hall.

At the Guia chapel, Christiansen beat on a sheet of metal with a hammer, worked a set of bells and said, 'What time is it — is it what time — time is it what?' and so on, marking time by asking questions about it. Meanwhile, Nørgaard created a table object with plaster, twelve cups and seven roses. He pricked his finger and let a drop of blood fall into each of the cups, cut the roses off the stems and cast the flowers into the audience. Outside the chapel, a heavy 240 kg cast iron 'cross' was propped up against the wall, which the two of them carried down to the river. On the riverbank, Nørgaard created heaps of salt and put a fish and a loaf of bread on top of each of them. On a previously prepared chair or throne, he created a plaster ramp to cover the stairs leading up to the throne, crawled up and spilt various materials (flour, salt, water, syrup, bread, fish, rose, egg) down it. Twelve pieces of sacking cloth were lying by the water, which Nørgaard dipped in the river and beat on the rocks. Christiansen wrote the Japanese sign for 'peace' on the rocks with yellow paint. After having set fire to a boat, they walked up to the bridge, Christiansen carrying a white banner, once again with the word 'peace' written on it, which he threw into the water. Nørgaard let a white dove loose in the middle of the bridge.

Inside the grotto, Nørgaard repeated the action from MANRESA, where he cast his feet in plaster. He walked up to the church altar in his plaster feet and started creating a bed of clay, broken glass and syrup. He also created a landscape consisting of twelve heaps of gravel with twelve mirrors embedded in them, then broke an egg over each mirror. Meanwhile, Christiansen performed his *180 Hammer Blows Against War Monkeys (Mongers)* by hammering 180 times on a sheet of metal. He performed/played most of his contributions to MANRESA, including *Eurasian Staff, 82min Fluxorum Organum*, *Ikke/kan* and *Knocking*, displayed the text 'Save the nature – use FLUXUS', blew on a birdsong whistle and played *Water Music* with his bells. In the meeting hall, Mennekes read a text, interrupted by sounds from Christiansen, while Nørgaard handed out bread and fried fish.

Before the performance, on 23 October 1994, Nørgaard was asked by the organisers to explain his contribution. He wrote back that it was 'almost impossible' for him to explain his part of the action and that anyhow, 'what should be left should only be what is left in the minds of the people who will be present during our action'.[20] Despite his misgivings, however, he did send an explanation, and it does a lot to clarify his thoughts. One thing it certainly does, is to explain Nørgaard's views on the relation between religion or spirituality and the everyday. The table/altar at La Guia, for example, was described by him as 'the dining table, the working table, the altar, the last supper.' It was intended to communicate the continuity between everyday actions (eating, working) and spirituality. He explained the roses as a reference to love, the crown of thorns and Beuys's use of roses in his actions. The twelve cups stood for twelve persons: the Apostles, who received the blood of Christ during the Last Supper. Setting fire to the boat by the river, he wrote, was a literal 'enlightenment', but also a reference to Viking raids and burials. The ramp he built, leading to the throne, was designed to suggest Jacob's ladder, the road to enlightenment, but also a pulpit and, via that association, the Sermon on the Mount. The washing and beating of the sacking was a reference to John the Baptist and baptism as a symbol of membership of a spiritual community. In each case, base materials were used to suggest spiritual values and biblical or historical references.

Apart from explaining some of the references, Nørgaard also touches upon the artistic side of his imagery. Working with plaster, for example, is discussed by him in terms of formless material — water and minerals/earth — being moulded in a distinct form by means of the hands. The rose has already been mentioned as a reference to Beuys, but Nørgaard also wrote in his explanation that Beuys had probably wanted him to perform his Sculptural Demonstrations during MANRESA 'as an example how an artist through "artistic" or "spiritual" exercises can work with art in a new way', so the historical reference to MANRESA should be considered a layer of meaning as well. The bed he built was a reference to Beuys as well: it referred to his sickness and death, as well as to Ignatius lying wounded in the city of Manresa and to dreams and meditation. There are also plenty of references to his own work. He does not mention them explicitly, but the bed, the boat, the bird for the Holy Spirit and the fish for Christ, the light bulbs, the plaster, the gravel, the mirrors, the syrup and the eggs were all materials and symbols he had used before. The many layers of meaning make it veritably impossible to fully unpack them all, but the symbolism will be clear to most observers: the wet plaster that solidifies, versus the shapeless heaps of gravel and the hard, frigid surfaces of the mirrors; the modelling of the clay contrasting the breaking of the lightbulbs; the sugary sweet energy of the syrup, against the latent life of the egg, and so on.

Christiansen never supplied an explanation like Nørgaard's, but in the context of his work, it is possible to hazard a calculated guess. His sound-making at the edge of the natural and the artificial can be seen to echo Nørgaard's play with amorphous materials and sculptural gestures. The text 'Save the nature – use FLUXUS' serves to underline this particular associative chain, but also extends it to Beuysian thought, where one of the connotations of the word 'fluxus' is the back-and-forth between East and West and between spirit and reason. His hammer strokes against warmongers produced unpredictable over and undertones too rich for the human ear, so they felt like a physical attack, but he composed works for a 'stupid hammer', a 'clever hammer' and a 'peaceful hammer' as well. This means that his hammer works need to be situated somewhere between the blow and the ringing of a church bell, between war and peace. In a similarly ambiguous way, the Japanese sign for 'peace' was written with yellow paint, which in Christiansen's universe of signs and meanings stands for the canary, the caged bird at the edge between nature and culture. The white banner, finally, can be read as a symbol of peace as well as an empty page that could carry any message one might wish to share with one's fellow humans.

Thinking, acting and travelling together

By means of this back and forth of meanings, Christiansen and Nørgaard shaped *Manresa Hbf* as everything but a main station. What they created was a maze of tracks running through the city of Manresa, through history, art history and religion, through their own oeuvres and through their understanding of that of Beuys. Specifically in relation to the latter, they managed to give living form to Christiansen's understanding of Beuys's thoughts and methods as expressed in 'Reality Multiplied by Three', the text from 1968 that was already briefly discussed in the introduction of this article. It is from this text that the phrase 'neither incorrect nor unimportant' comes. Christiansen chose this formulation to underline that he did not regard his interpretation as watertight and final: he did not write his text to explain Beuys once and for all, but because he thought his considerations were along the right track and important enough to share with others.

In the text, he presented four takes on Beuys, the first of which has to do with the way in which Beuys always opposes a phenomenon to its opposite, as in the conceptual pair *Raum* (space) and *Gegenraum* (counter-space). Christiansen chooses to interpret this as the opposition between a phenomenon as defined by external means (language and concepts) and the same phenomenon as it is experienced. Art is not identified with the one or the other, but is situated at the point where the two intersect, where they seem to be identical. The challenge for the artist is to find a method that can reach out to both sides, to the world of concepts and to the world of experience. Christiansen's second take on Beuys has to do with the way he uses his materials. Beuys, he says, does not force his material in a particular shape, but follows it. In accordance with his idea that Beuys tries to find a position where the same tools can address concept and experience alike, he concludes that Beuys chooses his material to address concepts as well as experiences. In other words, it should not be seen as a materialisation of an idea that is extraneous to it or as a pure experience, but as idea and experience rolled into one. Christiansen's third take on Beuys addresses the issue of imagery. Here, his conclusion is the same, namely, that recognisable images or symbols should not be seen as extraneous to the material and the processes used. Their meaning, he says, does not lie in the shape alone, but at least as much in the choice of material and the process that brings the image into being. Christiansen's fourth and last take has to do with the nature of Beuys's actions. Beuys's actions do not so much employ human beings, as take place inside human beings — performers as well as spectators. It would be wrong, he says, to consider them as illustrations of a principle by means of living bodies — as theatre — because it is much more important that the concepts that are addressed unfold themselves inside the minds and do their work there.

Christiansen and Nørgaard ended up working along exactly these lines, each in their own fashion. *Manresa Hbf* came about in a back-and-forth movement between the experience of the action itself as it unfolded and the concepts it activated. Materials, imagery and action all served to trigger associations in the spectator-participants: associations understood both as knowledge that is activated, experiences that are made meaningful and actions that invite action in the world, in accordance with the artists' references to peace, free speech, communality and man's ability to shape his/her own world. In the process, various themes are picked up that emerge from the two artists' dealings with Beuys: their contributions to the original MANRESA first and foremost, but also the hammer blows, the cross, the act of writing as a constitutive part of an action and so on.

However, there are also the last two sentences of 'Reality Multiplied by Three' to consider: 'The struggle or war between the material and spiritual ideas of humanity is something Joseph Beuys and Ignacio de Loyola shared in their will to pave the way for peaceful, dynamic humans. The halved cross — the two realities of humans — and Element 3!' Beuys and Ignatius, Christiansen says, are tied together by a path they chose. It is the path itself that is Element 3 from the original MANRESA. There is spirituality, there is rationality — and then there is the will to embark on the journey that will fuse the two. What *Manresa Hbf* added to MANRESA is a manifestation of precisely that journey. During the six hours of the action, on their way from station to station, Christiansen, Nørgaard and the audience travelled through a series of physical experiences and mental/conceptual vistas that weaved in and out of each other, with the discussion at the end as an opportunity to put into words what one had experienced on the way. If landscape and movement were only suggested in MANRESA, they were physically present in *Manresa Hbf*. The city of Manresa and its geography were included as anti-space to confront the space of the participants' culturally conditioned and historically determined reservoir of systems, knowledge and images. Christiansen ended his text from 1968: with the words, 'I am flying to you too, MANRESA.' In *Manresa Hbf*, these words are supplemented with 'by means of you I think, MANRESA', 'within and with you I work, MANRESA' and 'through you I travel, MANRESA.'

1
In German: '...nicht unrichtig und vor allem auch nicht unwichtig'. Henning Christiansen, 'Die Wirklichkeit mal 3: 4 Episteln über Joseph Beuys Arbeitsmethoden', 1968, Henning Christiansen Archive, Askeby (DK), in this publication (p. 66).

2
Another reason why this article can have no claim to 'the truth' is that I have never witnessed any of the actions discussed. What is presented as fact is actually based on eyewitness accounts, and as experience varies from person to person, one always has to allow for flaws and mis-recollections.

3
Hans-Jørgen Nielsen, 'Efter zero', *Dansk Musiktidsskrift* (DMT), no. 7, 1965, pp. 213–215.

4
Joseph Beuys, letter to Henning Christiansen, 20 November 1966. Henning Christiansen Archive, Møn, correspondence box 8.

5
In his first transcriptions of the sound fragment, Christiansen does not use the question mark, which causes the sentence to read as 'Now has Element 2 climbed up...' and so on. At some point, Beuys corrected the transcription as it appeared in the Ex-Schools's magazine *ta'*, adding the question mark, but it remains uncertain when exactly this happened. Much later, Christiansen acknowledged that the version with the question mark was the correct one.

6
In a note dated 9 February 1997, Christiansen explained the reference to the Thorvaldsen Museum. After *Tilstande*, he writes that the participants wandered around in the area surrounding the museum and left messages in chalk saying, 'they went that way'. Meanwhile, they discussed the sculpture of Thorvaldsen, marble's 'classical clarity', coldness, and so on. Note in Henning Christiansen Archive, Møn, correspondence box 9, HC + Beuys 1.

7
Hans-Jørgen Nielsen, *At det at. Et læsealbum*. Copenhagen: Borgen, 1965, n. p.

8
In an undated CV, datable to 1969, for example, he describes his work both as 'visual music' and 'imaginary architecture'. Henning Christiansen Archive, Møn, correspondence box 7.

9
Score/description in Henning Christiansen Archive, correspondence box 7. It is by no means certain that the actions were performed in precisely this order, but as there are too few witness statements to confirm or correct Nørgaard's list, for the sake of clarity I have chosen to let it stand uncommented.

10
Henning Christiansen, 'Også en falsk interpretation (I II III IV)' / 'Die Wirklichkeit mal 3: 4 Episteln über Joseph Beuys Arbeitsmethoden'. Manuscript in Danish and German, 1968. Henning Christiansen Archive, Møn, correspondence box 9.

11
February–July 1967, November 1967–February 1968, October 1968–March 1969 and April–May 1969.

12
Christiansen, quoted in Uwe M. Schneede, *Joseph Beuys: die Aktionen*. Ostfildern-Ruit: Gerhard Hatje, 1994, p. 167.

13
Dejligt vejr i dag/Schönes Wetter heute – n'est-ce pas – Ibsen. Kammeropera/ritual/messe/oratorium. Music: Henning Christiansen. Libretto: Hans-Jørgen Nielsen. Scenography and actors: Bjørn Nørgaard. Copenhagen 1968, p. 2.

14
Joseph Beuys quoted in Mario Kramer, *Joseph Beuys. Das Kapital Raum 1970–1977*. Heidelberg: Edition Staeck 1991, p. 27.

15
Henning Christiansen, 'En rapport for at finde ud af hvorfor og hvordan jeg lever og hvad det er der interesserer mig' (A report to find out why and how I live and what it is that interests me), 7 June 1971, Henning Christiansen Archive, Møn, box 66, texts by and on HC 1.

16
Henning Christiansen, 'Die grosse grüne Zelt-Symphonie (mit Vögeln)', 1980. Henning Christiansen Archive, Møn, folder 'Opus 133'.

17
Henning Christiansen, 'Fra action til production', Ellen Tange Mortensen *et al.* (eds.), *Bjørn Nørgaard –Objekt, skulptur –tableau*. Aarhus: Aarhus Kunstmuseum, 1986, pp. 35–42.

18
Description based on Bjørn Nørgaard, 'To play To day - Et tilbageblik på i morgen', *Dansk Musiktidsskrift* (DMT), vol. 61, no. 4, 1987, pp. 184–189.

19
Henning Christiansen to Poul Kock, 30 March 1988. Henning Christiansen Archive, box 'Opus 158: Tiefland'.

20
Bjørn Nørgaard, fax to Pilar Parcerisas, 23 October 1994, Henning Christiansen Archive, Møn, folder 'Projects 1994–1995'.

PILAR PARCERISAS

A JOURNEY AND AN INVOCATION

'Mysteries take place at the central station, not at Goetheanum'.[1] Joseph Beuys

In the middle of the 1960s and in the context of the Fluxus movement, Joseph Beuys found that upending the art system could be an artistic discipline. Art could be an instrument for changing man and the world, but to do this it would be necessary to broaden its narrow constraints and expand the concept itself: all of Beuys's actions 'were important for expanding the old concept of art. For broadening and expanding it whenever possible, so that it might include any human activity.'[2]

Various actions in that period staged initiation voyages, spells or invocations, which through ritual forms were focused on activating a special energy to enable the transformation of a space into a magical site, of entirely changing a line of thought or of creating new lines of interpretation for the relationship between man and the world. These rituals have been compared with the technique of ecstasy in shamans, and could be 'outings to points of magical Flight.'[3] Thus, as Beuys would write on the script for the action MANRESA / *Homage to Schmela* (Galerie Schmela, 21 February 1966), 'Auch zu dir fliege ich, MANRESA' [I am flying to you too, MANRESA]. Manresa was thus a city as well as a hot spot for spiritual geography and transformational, curative energy.

The spiritual substrate of Beuys's action MANRESA lay in Ignatius of Loyola, who the artist read and reread during his spiritual crisis of the 1950s. Loyola lead church renewal, creating the Company of Jesus. Having left his weapons aside after being wounded in a battle, with the idea of turning himself into a pilgrim, he created an army of soul transformers, activating individual self-determination and setting out its theoretical and practical foundations in the *Spiritual Exercises*, which he wrote in Manresa during his stage in the city from 1622 to 1623, after a previous and rather illuminating visit to Montserrat. Beuys found in Loyola's life a biographical parallel with his own: the crash of his military plane near Crimea in 1943, the wounds and pains he would endure for the rest of his life, and the shifted focus of art as socially transformative, required to follow the principle of freedom[4] and of self-determination, so that all this could be poured into his forms of social art.

To a certain degree, the action MANRESA opens the doors for Beuys, following the example of Loyola, in the evolution of his work towards social sculpture. The mystery of this action lies in the question 'Where is Element 3?', a phrase repeatedly invoked in the script. Beuys responds to this query on 22 June 1967, when founding the German Students Party as a meta-party in Room 13 of the Staatlische Kunstakademie in Düsseldorf. This would be Beuys's first disembarkation in the political arena, when he decided to undertake a crusade, grounded in art, for social, political and economic change. The Jesuit Friedhelm Mennekes has studied more than anyone else the symbolism of the action MANRESA, the parallels between Beuys and Loyola and how each overcame respective personal crises; he also focused on the 'Christic' ritual contained in this action and what it means as an activation of the will of Christ and point of inflexion for the highest ideal of Beuysian thought: 'social sculpture'.[5]

Manresa, Central Station

The action *Manresa Hbf*, which was carried out in the city of Manresa on 4 November 1994 by the composer-musician Henning Christiansen and the sculptor Bjørn Nørgaard, Danish creators who had worked closely with Joseph Beuys on the original action MANRESA/*Homage to Schmela* (1966), upholds the spiritual substrate of the earlier action-demonstration, as well as that of Loyola himself at Manresa. It transforms the site into an authentic 'central station', a place where mysteries take place.

The corresponding exhibition, which brought together the majority of drawings and photographs from the action MANRESA (1966), was held at the Sala Plana de l'Om of the Fundació Caixa de Manresa, in Manresa. It was open from 4 to 27 November 1994 in Manresa, and from 17 January to 5 March 1995, at the Centre d'Art Santa Mònica, in Barcelona. In Manresa the exhibition was presented with a lecture by Harald Szeemann. The title of the show was *Manresa Hauptbahnhof*, coinciding with the name of the action.

Once the show had opened, I received a letter from Dieter Koepplin, who I had sent the catalogue to. He praised the catalogue texts, including my own, entitled 'I am flying to you too, MANRESA', where I mention the importance of the Tort Cross for the action MANRESA; this in turn reminded him of a trip he had made to Manresa due to his interest in Beuys.[6] In that text I cited Heiner Bastian, who in turn recalled the phrase of Beuys, 'Mysteries take place at the central station', which is repeated in various texts on Beuys. Yet this phrase has been cut, so Koepplin sent me as well the full interview done by Peter Brugge with Joseph Beuys in *Der Spiegel*. Here is the full exchange: 'SPIEGEL: Perhaps people are frightened by the mystical and shamanistic aspects of your actions and work, the appearance of alchemical and mythical signs, while in contrast for advanced followers of anthroposophy they are familiar. BEUYS: Mysteries take place at the central station, not at Goetheanum'.[7] With this Beuys sought to say, according to Koepplin in his letter, that 'true "mysteries" are not found in places like the Goetheanum of the Anthroposophical Society (which was built by Steiner near Basel), but rather in a train station, at work places, in factories, etc.'[8] Beuys distanced himself from Rudolf Steiner while exploring a cartography of possible stations with the potential for movement, impulse and transformation that could occur wherever possible, places where man might make the choice to accept the impulse of Christ and free himself from materialism. Manresa, as a site, is one of these possible stations, something Ignatius of Loyola's transformation provided confirmation of.

In the action *Manresa Hbf* (1994), this journey comes to fruition. Using different instruments, an invocation is fulfilled with the site's strength and energy, a *Braunraum*, a brown space, in the mystical geography of the Christ on the Tort Cross. This relief sculpture had become a mystical mandorla, the medallion from the wayside cross that is now at the Saint Ignatius Cave, which sweated blood in 1627. I recall the surprised look on the faces of Christiansen and Nørgaard when we saw this cross. At almost the same moment, they remarked how sure they were that Beuys had been there and seen that Christ. No doubt, there is a resemblance between the Christ on the Tort Cross and the plate with a Christ done in putty that Beuys used in the action MANRESA, as well as the detail on the windows of Galerie Schmela, where he had written the word BARCELONA, thus specifying the place the action refers to.

During the preparation of this project, the first central station I found was at Darmstadt, where the Block Beuys is held at the Hessisches Landesmuseum Darmstadt. This body of work is a compendium of residual objects from his actions as brought together by the collector Ströher; objects from the action MANRESA (1966) also feature. This body of material had been shown as part of the Joseph Beuys retrospective at the Städtisches Museum Abteiberg in Monchengladbach (1967), while the objects from the action MANRESA were seen at the 1968 Kassel documenta. In the train station, the old tin sign reading DARMSTADT HBF, in white and blue, gave me the idea of creating a similar sign to turn Manresa (site, action and exhibition all in one) into a central station: MANRESA HBF.

I have said above that the action *Manresa Hbf* was the fulfilment of a voyage and an invocation, a visitation to the original energy source for two artists who were the mediators and conductors of this north-south journey in the Eurasian continent. There is a drawing by Joseph Beuys on the back of an envelope entitled *N/S/E/O* [North, South, East, West] (1966), which sketches out a European cross, with Rome and Manresa to the south and Denmark to the north; three branches reach out to three Scandinavian countries, Norway, Sweden

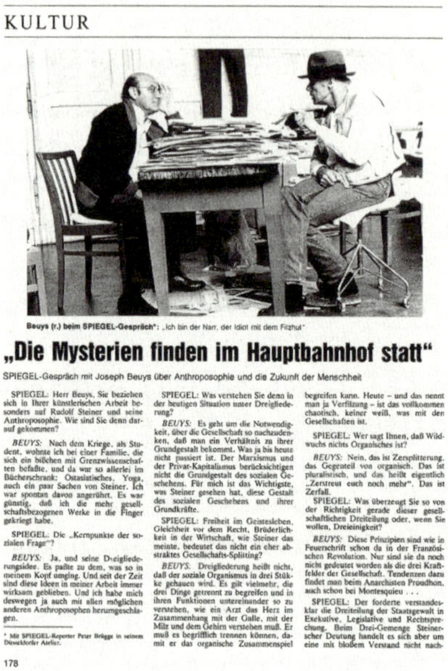

KULTUR

Beuys (r.) beim SPIEGEL-Gespräch*: „Ich bin der Narr, der Idiot mit dem Filzhut"

„Die Mysterien finden im Hauptbahnhof statt"

SPIEGEL-Gespräch mit Joseph Beuys über Anthroposophie und die Zukunft der Menschheit

SPIEGEL: Herr Beuys, Sie beziehen sich in Ihrer künstlerischen Arbeit besonders auf Rudolf Steiner und seine Anthroposophie. Wie sind Sie denn darauf gekommen?

BEUYS: Nach dem Kriege, als Student, wohnte ich bei einer Familie, die sich ein bißchen mit Grenzwissenschaften befaßte, und da war so allerlei im Bücherschrank: Ostasiatisches, Yoga, auch ein paar Sachen von Steiner. Ich war spontan davon angerührt. Es war günstig, daß ich die mehr gesellschaftsbezogenen Werke in die Finger gekriegt habe.

SPIEGEL: Die „Kernpunkte der sozialen Frage"?

BEUYS: Ja, und seine Dreigliederungsidee. Es paßte zu dem, was so in meinem Kopf umging. Und seit der Zeit sind diese Ideen in meiner Arbeit immer wirksam geblieben. Und ich habe mich deswegen ja auch mit allen möglichen anderen Anthroposophen herumgeschlagen.

SPIEGEL: Was verstehen Sie denn in der heutigen Situation unter Dreigliederung?

BEUYS: Es geht um die Notwendigkeit, über die Gesellschaft so nachzudenken, daß man ein Verhältnis zu ihrer Grundgestalt bekommt. Was ja bis heute nicht passiert ist. Der Marxismus und der Privat-Kapitalismus berücksichtigen nicht die Grundgestalt des sozialen Geschehens. Für mich ist das Wichtigste, was Steiner gesehen hat, diese Gestalt des sozialen Geschehens und ihrer Grundkräfte.

SPIEGEL: Freiheit im Geistesleben, Gleichheit vor dem Recht, Brüderlichkeit in der Wirtschaft, wie Steiner das meinte, bedeutet das nicht ein eher abstraktes Gesellschafts-Splitting?

BEUYS: Dreigliederung heißt nicht, daß der soziale Organismus in drei Stükke gehauen wird. Es gilt vielmehr, die drei Dinge getrennt zu begreifen und in ihren Funktionen untereinander so zu verstehen, wie ein Arzt das Herz im Zusammenhang mit der Galle, mit der Milz und dem Gehirn verstehen muß. Er muß es begrifflich trennen können, damit er das organische Zusammenspiel begreifen kann. Heute – und das nennt man ja Verfilzung – ist das vollkommen chaotisch, keiner weiß, was mit den Gesellschaften ist.

SPIEGEL: Wer sagt Ihnen, daß Wildwuchs nichts Organisches ist?

BEUYS: Nein, das ist Zersplitterung, das Gegenteil von organisch. Das ist pluralistisch, und das heißt eigentlich „Zerstreut euch noch mehr". Das ist Zerfall.

SPIEGEL: Was überzeugt Sie so von der Richtigkeit gerade dieser gesellschaftlichen Dreiteilung oder, wenn Sie wollen, Dreieinigkeit?

BEUYS: Diese Prinzipien sind wie in Feuerschrift schon da in der Französischen Revolution. Nur sind sie da noch nicht gedeutet worden als die drei Kraftfelder der Gesellschaft. Tendenzen dazu findet man beim Anarchisten Proudhon, auch schon bei Montesquieu . . .

SPIEGEL: Der forderte verstandesklar die Dreiteilung der Staatsgewalt in Exekutive, Legislative und Rechtsprechung. Beim Drei-Gemenge Steinerscher Deutung handelt es sich aber um eine mit bloßem Verstand nicht nach-

* Mit SPIEGEL-Reporter Peter Brügge in seinem Düsseldorfer Atelier.

178

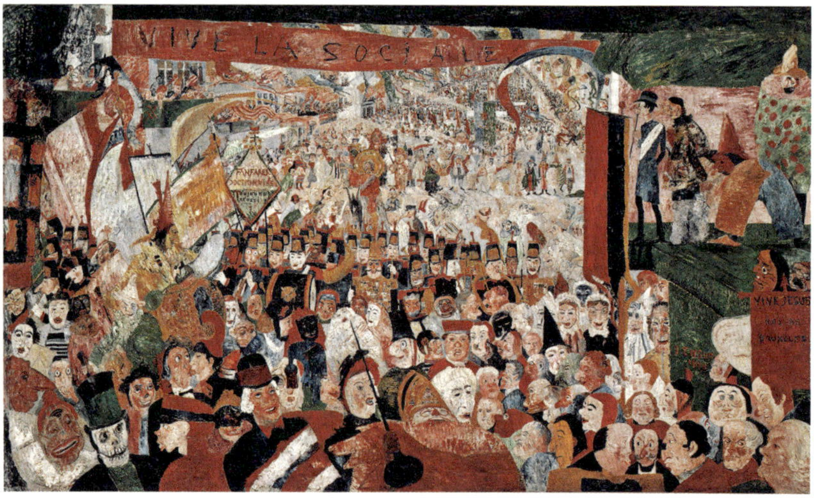

A 'Die Mysterien finden im Hauptbahnhof statt', Peter Brügge interview with Joseph Beuys, *Der Spiegel*, 23, 1984.

B James Ensor, *Christ's Entry into Brussels in 1889*, 1888.

and Finland, as if they were three rivers[9]. Beside this, two squares touching on one corner encircle an M (Manresa) and a K (København). Another horizontal pencil line crosses from east to west. On one end is written 'Asia' and on the other 'Ostend', which means the end of the east.[10] For Beuys that is where the earth ends (if we take into account that for him it was where the Eurasian continent ended). When in Ostend, Beuys was not going to miss the James Ensor painting *Christ's Entry into Brussels in 1889* (1888), a piece that situates religion, politics and art, with the Christ figure in the centre as a kind of self-portrait, surrounded by a crowd of dehumanised individuals. The subject of this painting runs parallel somewhat to the scenario of social art that Beuys envisioned in making a better society. In the action MANRESA he activates the will of Christ to accomplish this. Christiansen tells the story of how in a visit to Ostend, Beuys told him about his affinities with Ensor; they visited his tomb and Beuys explained the *Western Man Project*, which he wanted to build over the waters.[11]

This cross drawing has the form of a European man, a European cross, with two feet in the south: Rome, representing classicism, and Manresa, being intuition and light. Beuys equates Manresa (M) with Copenhagen (K), as two spaces that are counter-fields one to the other, two *Braunräume*, two brown spaces. In Copenhagen we find the Thorvaldsen Museum, dedicated to the sculptor who spent years of his life in Rome, invoked in the action MANRESA. Beuys believes that it is the furthest away classicism reaches, and with it the intuition of the south. Three small crosses of a similar nature pulsate in the shape of a man for the drawing, while a cross broken in half stands out in the right-hand margin of the drawing. The eastern part of the cross is ignored, which is left to western man to construct so as to unite Occident with Orient. From the transept of this cross a line emerges horizontally and crosses through one of these men, which at the same time are lines of geographical, cultural and anthropological energy.

After the action MANRESA, Beuys and Christiansen carried out the action *Eurasian Staff, 82 min Fluxorum Organum* on 2 July 1967, in Vienna's Galerie nächst St. Stephan. In this action, the north-south verticality is completed horizontally with the Eurasian staff, which activates the east-west axis. From this point on, Beuys appears as a pilgrim and spiritual guide for a policy of liberation, emancipation and union of Eastern spirituality with the analytic science of Western man. Yet Vienna is also a city on the limits of the eastern world: 'Vienna is a city which is deeply permeated with the colouring of Eastern Europe', observes Nam June Paik.[12] On 9 February 1968, the action *Eurasian Staff* was held again at the new Wide White Space Gallery, run by Anny de Decker and Bernd Lohaus in Antwerp. In a certain sense, with these two actions in two cities representing the east and west of the Eurasian continent, the horizontal axis of the cross in the Beuys drawing had been realised.

Nevertheless, the north-south journey as signified in the action *Manresa Hbf* (1994) had not yet been fulfilled. This action was in no way a repetition of MANRESA. The event upholds the nomadic spirit of the actions of Beuys. The two Danish artists made the north-south journey physically, like two pilgrims, and created a new liturgy in homage to Beuys and Ignatius of Loyola. To a certain degree, their action activated anew the will of Christ, with the power of the site at the central station of Ignatius of Loyola. One of the Christiansen scores speaks of the traveller (*Der Reisende*) and the wounded man (*Der Verbundete*); it also addresses man's effort to overcome materialism and positivism and so activate what drives each individual to draw nearer to Christ through matter and be transformed into a new man, into the New Cross. The effort involved is enormous, and for this reason Christiansen's Score VI has a repetition in Danish: '*Ikke kann, kann ikke – kann kann ikke ikke...*' (Can't do it, do it can't, can, can, can't can't). The composition accompanies a sculptural action by Nørgaard. In the piece, the sculptor submerged his feet in wet plaster; once the material had solidified, he tried to walk with his coffered feet. This was the Danish sculptor's contribution to the action in Copenhagen (Gallery 101, 1966), as well as to MANRESA (1966), *Manresa* (1991) and *Manresa Hbf* (1994).

The two wounded travellers in the Christiansen score are Beuys and Loyola. The splitting of contemporary man into Western and Eastern, dividing the reason and intuition that Joseph Beuys had proposed in the original MANRESA action, also is related to a split in Europe and a divided Germany, a traumatic state he felt in his own body. Beuys describes himself as someone 'born of a wound'[13]: 'The desire to reach beyond the wound and the deep spiritual breach, the moral trauma, was at the root of his nature art; it determined his course and the role his drawings played in it.'[14]

Christ and Brown Spaces

In their action, Christiansen and Nørgaard did not use objects or texts from the first MANRESA, despite the fact that the script has been published and is signed by all three. There was no felt, no fat, no copper, nor any other identifiable material with the language of Joseph Beuys. Christiansen and Nørgaard only sought to be transmitters of a message with their own language and tools, with the music and the sculptural material in a holy land, where ritual might be effective: a *Braunraum*. It is indeed true that Manresa is geographically a brown space, for the colour of the clay earth that surround the River Cardener, and for the erosion of the river which has created shaped rises with the sediments on the river bank, with perforations or caves which are known there as *balmes*. It is an eminently sculptural landscape, dominated by grey, brown and green on the sides of the river, a unique landscape that in ancient times was known as the Valley of Paradise. Yet it is also a space where it has been demonstrated that transubstantiation is possible.

Beuys's brown crosses (*Braunkreuze*) have an earthy red tone, distinguished by a 'certain balance between numbed earthliness and flowing blood. They represent the process of incarnation, where material receives the spirit. They also resonate with the Catholic term used by Beuys of "transubstantiation"'.[15] Let us recall once again that the Christ of the medallion on the Tort Cross perspired blood in 1627. On 4 November 1994, during the presentation of the action *Manresa Hbf*, a massive downpour emptied the sky and turned the Cardener Valley and the river water itself into a veritable brown space. The forces of nature accompanied the activation of the will of Christ from the beginning of the action in the Nostra Senyora de la Guia Shrine, and the second stage of the action in the caves of the Cardener, followed by a thousand spectators.

Beuys defined the will of Christ as a potential force that has been in the world ever since the crucifixion,[16] although it also has an evolutive meaning. Evolution and potentiality are two faces of the same coin. In his drawing *Evolution* (1974), the Sun is related to Jupiter and to the principle of heat ('Sonnenstaat', 'Jupiter', 'Wärmefähre') while the name of Christ is related to the term 'Placenta'. Certain lines intersect from these two poles, creating wellsprings of energy.

Potentiality comes into play in every one of the artist's action, and MANRESA is no exception. In the later action *Manresa Hbf* (1994), these messages are enhanced in an evolutive, potential manner, although employing other instruments and a different liturgy. The original message is expanded and made to resonate. For Beuys, evolution is a concept linked to 'metamorphosis, transubstantiation, transformation, the heat principle or the will of Christ.'[17] Beuys calls on the individual, giving each person responsibility to continue the course of creation on earth through individual transformation, leaving behind the material and embracing the spiritual, so that it might contribute in this way to the transformation of the planet until 'the very social substance is converted into a solar State, that is, that it might be the planet of the future where people work and carry out their affairs in other conditions of life, of a more elevated nature.'[18]

All of this is related in turn to Rudolf Steiner and the interpretation anthroposophy offers for the Mystery of Golgotha, with death as the beginning of life. As Max Reithmann observes, 'heat, light and corporeality are conceived as a spiritual activity that characterises man as a creating being.'[19] The heat principle will in this way govern the concept of 'evolution'. Christ is the principle of heat assimilated into the Sun. Rudolf Steiner reworks the beginning of the Evangels: 'In the beginning was the Word (*Logos*)...' The highest spirit is connected with the Sun and who sends the "I" to Earth is called in occult teaching Christ. The "I", as members of the solar Logos, gradually flowed and penetrated into forms. Light shines from the solar Logos, yet in ancient times very few were able to receive this light. Those who in contrast were able to receive it became different than those beside them. In this way they were called 'children of God' or 'sons of god' (Ch. 1, 12)[20] For Steiner, 'the most important event for the evolution of the cosmos and man was the event of Golgotha.'[21] Anthroposophy here spreads word of this mystery:[22] 'Given that the Light of Christ irradiates from Earth, there is a kind of reflection that circles the Earth. What is reflected as the Light of Christ and appears as the event of Golgotha is what was called the Holy Spirit. Just as the event of Golgotha constituted the first Impulse for the Earth to be transformed into Sun, since then the Earth has become creative, surrounding itself with a spiritual ring which in the future will convert into a kind of planet that will revolve around the Earth.'[23] The agonising Christ thus gives rise to a new Sun, so that the Earth might advance in the path of 'evolution'. In these arguments, anthroposophy is made manifest not as a religion but as a path of knowledge that seeks to lead the spiritual in man towards the spiritual in the universe.

There are other references to Steiner that intermittently appear and reappear in the work of Joseph Beuys over the course of his career, such as the example of a triadic system grounded in alchemy (sulphur, salt and mercury), the triple structure of the social organism (legal, economic and cultural), the personal triad (head, heart, body) and a fourth human principle: the I, intimately related to blood, which is where potentiality is found.

The action MANRESA (1966) invokes the Mystery of Golgotha, an event which symbolically unites the blood of Christ with the earth. Its Trinitarian character puts into play Element 1 (the Father), Element 2 (the Son) and a third element, which is an unknown, although it does coincide with the solar ring that gives light to the earth amidst darkness, taking the name of the Holy Spirit. In the end, Element 3 is where social sculpture is developed. Beuys understands how to simultaneously utilise and flee from Steiner's referents in creating his own language, ritually assisted in this case by Christiansen's space of sound and musical scores and the sculptural contribution of Nørgaard.

A love and death machine

Mechanical features, batteries, electricity and heat conductors are components Beuys uses in his sculptures, and they also appear in the action MANRESA. He himself defined the Christ figure as 'the inventor of the steam engine', 'the Third Principle of Thermodynamics' or as 'electricity'.[24] In this action, Beuys faces the divided cross with a challenge to overcome, and calls on contemporary man to use the impulse of Christ to reunify this fragmented cross and transform it into a New Cross, into a new man who in his union with the cosmos might alter our future on Earth. This he does by activating various factors: a solar disc, the photograph of a generator, the ears and innards of a hare, bicycle pumps, a plate with an image of Christ in plaster, a milk bottle and another of lead, a bird, a toy ambulance, a high-tension generator and a Geissler tube full of neon gas that lights up when rubbing against textile, creating energy between his heart and the plate with the plaster Christ. The impulse, therefore, is facilitated with electrical energy created with everyday objects.

Mennekes had described and defined with great precision the steps of the action and the movement of its components. The machine works, as it is a machine of love and death. As if Beuys had activated a *machine célibataire*, which from now on could be run all by itself, without its guide, in function of the principle of self-determination of each individual. A shift of energy and functions has taken place, the demonstration has been carried out. MANRESA is an 'action-demonstration', as with other actions from the mid-1960s, that can be related to each other in certain aspects: *Eurasia* (1963), *How to Explain Pictures to a Dead Hare* (1965), MANRESA (1966), *Eurasian Staff* (1967), *Hauptstrom* (1967) and *Vacuum–Mass* (1968). The ritual of MANRESA further constitutes a call to make sculpture invisible, so that it might be nothing other than social sculpture, that which is hidden behind each individual: 'everyone is an artist, in potential', is the famous Beuys statement, along with 'creativity is capital'.

Manresa Hbf (1994) signified the expansion or broadening of the action MANRESA, enabled by the spirit of Fluxus and by its memory. It made it possible for the lesson and spirit of the master to make it to the holy Ignatian sites of the city of Manresa, as expressed by his closest collaborators. This memory is brought together in the divided cross made from cast iron created by Bjørn Nørgaard, which made the journey from Denmark to Manresa and is now installed beneath the city's old Roman bridge, near the caves on the banks of the River Cardener.

To a certain degree, this cross has given a semantic quality to public space, in a spiritual sense, emerging as a new wayside cross along the River Cardener. Wayside crosses in Catalonia and the south of Europe in general did not only mark out the limits of a territory, property or parish. They were also blessed or could become references for shared religiosity, or demarcate a Christian territory. In this case, it is a cross for Ignatian and Beuysian devotion in the city of Manresa, in homage to Ignatius of Loyola and to Joseph Beuys, for what he was able to gather from Ignatian doctrine and apply from the perspective of art.

This cross has incrusted in it the memory of material used in MANRESA and its meaning in homage to Beuys and Loyola. Twelve electric bulbs hang off of it, referring back to the electrical apparatus used by Beuys in 1966, and related in turn to the twelve apostles. Along the horizontal axis, on the right, there is a small cross that is added as number thirteen, alluding to Christ and the crucifixion. This in turn is topped off by three light bulbs, a reference to the Holy Trinity. A bottle hangs from this horizontal cross, directly referring to Jesus on the cross, when he says 'Bring me a little water'.

Other objects refer to the parallels between Joseph Beuys and Ignatius of Loyola: a pilgrim's staff (the Eurasian staff), a soldier's rifle and a sword recall their common military pasts. Seven plates run from up from below along the vertical axis, each with a different symbol on it. Seven is a sacred number, which speaks to us of the seven heavens, or of the seven days of creation. On one of them we see the signature of Bjørn Nørgaard (Bjørn means "bear" in some Scandinavian languages), while on another there is the Greek cross used by Beuys as a signature on the stamp used by the German Students' Party (1967), the action *Hauptstrom* (1967) and in *Fluxus Zone West*, the name adopted by the students party in 1969. On another plate there is the Japanese sign for 'peace' used by Henning Christiansen, followed by another with Christ crucified on it, the emblem with the Christ from the Tort Cross and the plaster Christ on the plate that got MANRESA (1966) underway. Plate number five is printed with the image of a hare, while on the two plates at the top we encounter Element 1 and Element 2. Above these final plates, over them all, there is a kind of camping lamp used to light a path at night. This the light of the Holy Spirit, which guides our way in the darkness. With the cross by Nørgaard, the Celtic world has arrived to the south, to the Mediterranean, like a stake driven in the ground.

This cross has become an ongoing testimony to the action *Manresa Hbf* (1994) and a cautionary message that continues to speak to the man of today from Manresa, the central station. So as to find fulfilment for the European cross, as drawn by Beuys, we must take the same path in the opposite direction, from south to north. This is the will that had already been expressed by Henning Christiansen, which in turn has its own central station: the Thorvaldsen Museum in Copenhagen.

1
Peter Brügge, interview with Joseph Beuys, 'Die Mysterien finden im Hauptbahnhof statt', *Der Spiegel*, 23, 1984, p. 179.

2
Uwe M. Schneede takes this citation from Robert Filliou, *Lehren und Lernen als Aufführungskünste*, Cologne – New York: Verlag Gebrüder König, 1970, p. 161; in 'Acción', in *Beuysnobiscum*. In *Joseph Beuys*, Madrid: Museo Nacional Centro de Arte Reina Sofia, 1994, p. 241 [Exh. cat.].

3
Alois Martin Müller, 'Chamanes', in *Beuysnobiscum*, p. 255.

4
An ongoing point of reference for Joseph Beuys was the book by Rudolf Steiner, *The Philosophy of Freedom* (1893).

5
See Friedhelm Mennekes, *Beuys zu Christus/Beuys on Christ*, Stuttgart: Verlag Katolisches Bibelberk, 1989 and *Joseph Beuys Manresa. Eine Aktion als geistliche Übing nach Ignatius of Loyola*, Frankfurt am Main and Leipzig: Insel Verlag, 1992; *Joseph Beuys: Pensar Cristo*, Barcelona: Herder, 1997.

6
Letter from Dieter Koepplin to Pilar Parcerisas, Basel, 12 January 1995.

7
Brügge, 'Die Mysterien finden im Hauptbahnhof statt'.

8
Dieter Koepplin, op. cit. Original version: 'The true "Mysterienspiele" are not in such places like the Goetheanum of the Anthroposophical Society (near Basel, built by Rudolf Steiner), but in the railway station, in all working places, in factories, etc.).' This observation was also made by Franz Josef van der Grinten in 'Joseph Beuys as Nether-Rhinelander: A conversation with Franz Joseph Van der Grinten', in Joseph Beuys, *Greetings from the Eurasian*, Antwerp and London: M HKA and Koenig Books, 2017, p. 133 [Exh. cat.].

9
Pilar Parcerisas (ed.), *Manresa Hauptbahnhof*, Manresa: Fundació Caixa Manresa, 1994 [Exh. cat.], p. 104.

10
Henning Christiansen in *Joseph Beuys Eurasientab*, Antwerp: Galerie Anny de Decker, 1987, p. 89.

11
Pilar Parcerisas (ed.), *Joseph Beuys. MANRESA: A Spiritual Geography*, Barcelona: Tenov Books, 2021, p. 153.

12
Nam June Paik, 'Beuys weeds – Beuys creeds' (1984) (excerpt). In Joseph Beuys, *Greetings from the Eurasian*, p. 111 [Exh. cat.].

13
See the chronicle of his autobiographical narrative in *Life Course/Work Course*, 1964, p. 10.

14
Bernice Rose, 'Joseph Beuys and the Language of Drawing'. In *Thinking is Form: The Drawings of Joseph Beuys*, New York: MoMA, 1993, p. 78.

15
Doris Leutgeb, 'Cross', in *Beuysnobiscum*, p. 253.

16
Idem.

17
Kirsten Claudia Voigt, 'Evolución', in *Beuysnobiscum*, pp. 264–265.

18
Idem. Quote from the author of *Joseph Beuys. Aktive Neutralität. Die Überwindung von Kapitalismus und Kommunismus, Ein Vortrag mit Diskussion am 20. Januar 1985*, Düsseldorf: Wangen, 1985, p. 9.

19
Max Reithmann, *Joseph Beuys: La mort me tient en éveil*, Toulouse: ARPAP, 1994, p. 183.

20
Rudolf Steiner, 'First Lecture', Basel, 16 November 1907, in *Connaissance du Christ*, Geneva: Éditions Anthroposophiques Romandes, 1990, pp. 275–276.

21
Ibid., p. 276.

22
https://antroposofiahoy.jimdofree.com/misterio-del-gólgota [access: 16 October 2021]

23
Idem.

24
Doris Leutgeb, 'Christ (will of)', in *Beuysnobiscum*.

EPILOGUE

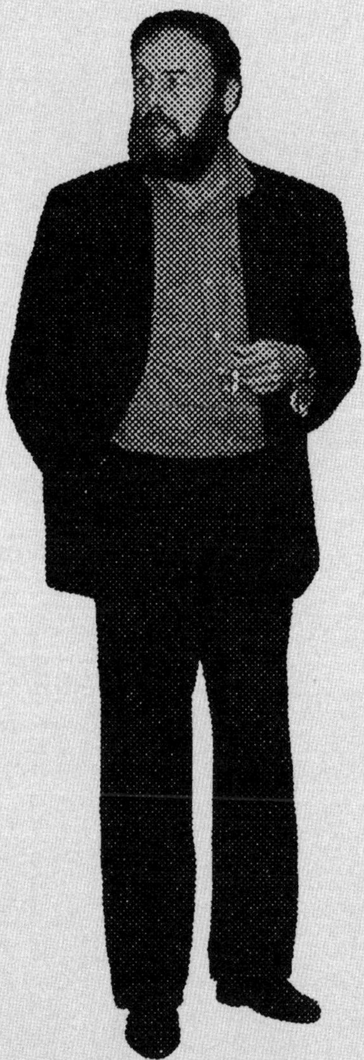

Lecture by Harald Szeemann on Joseph Beuys. Presented on 4 November 1994, at the Sala Plana de l'Om of the Fundació Caixa de Manresa, on the occasion of the inauguration of the exhibition *Joseph Beuys: Manresa Hauptbahnhof*, and the performance on the same day in the city of Manresa of the action *Manresa Hbf*, by Henning Christiansen and Bjørn Nørgaard.

Ladies and gentlemen,

It is a great honour for me to have been invited to participate in today's action in Manresa. I have been asked repeatedly today if the action is a repetition or a second version of the one that took place on 15 December 1966. I have answered that it is neither: in first regard, it is an homage to Beuys, but you will immediately observe that it is an homage charged with respect for the artist's work over the course of his career. Secondly, it is also an homage in recognition of two artists who participated in the original action, both of whom we have seen today, the composer Henning Christiansen and the sculptor Bjørn Nørgaard.

If you know about Beuys's work, you will have recognised certain characteristic traits of his oeuvre in the action that took place today. In the first station, there was always a moment when time was dragged out: time is expanded towards excess time; next, in the second station, what you saw at the river made reference to the Sermon on the Mount; in the third station, what you would have seen are the symbols Beuys used: the hare and the brown cross, as well as Element 1 and Element 2. As has already been mentioned, there were the shepherd's staff, the Eurasian staff, the air pump, and so on. At the end, then, everything came together at the church, both in terms of sound and material, as Beuys always said that without materialising, without entering into matter – and here I am speaking of the sculptor, but likewise of the spiritual Beuys – without this process it would not be possible to reach a higher state.

*

Anticipating a possible lack of knowledge of Beuys's work, I have thought that the best thing I might do would be to prepare a succinct presentation on various works by Beuys. I will try to keep myself to the time I have been granted by Pilar Parcerisas, who I would like to thank for recalling that she left this city when she was 22 years old, as I do believe that when a daughter returns in this way, it is something special both for her and the city itself.

*

The first piece I would like to comment on is *Room 563×491 ×563*, Künstlerhaus Nuremberg, 1968), which shows the treatment of a material that the two artists in the *Manresa Hbf* action did not use today. I refer to fat: Beuys spoke of fat as the authentic material of visual process. For him, in its warmest state, fat expresses form in a chaotic state; in a cold state, in turn, it represents spirituality. Between these two poles there is the sculptor's movement, which raises the chaos to a spiritual level where emotions come into play. In this way, everything that fascinated him about life, and everything that fascinated him on a spiritual level – the Trinity, mystery, yet material process as well – was divided into these three steps, for ultimately he sought to carry out these three principles of the human being, these three fundamental human freedoms: liberty, equality, fraternity. In his work these features are constituted, and they were always connected at every level he worked on. The sound we have heard during the action *Manresa Hbf*[1] is a recording that was done during the process of an action, but which later would be fixed as an artistic form in the museum. Combined with this tape recording, which was used today in the church, his reiterative sound refers to this relationship with the whole, which is needed to come to a new beginning. This 'Ja, ja, ja, ja' (Yes, yes, yes, yes) and 'Nee, nee, nee, nee' (No, no, no, no) is precisely the affirmation and negation of the critical spirit, which must rule out the preterite in affirming the new.

*

1. This refers to *Yes, Yes, Yes, Yes, Yes, No, No, No, No, No*, a sound recording of a Fluxus action that Beuys and Christiansen did with Johannes Stüttgen in December 1968 at the Kunstakademie Düsseldorf. For almost an entire hour, the three of them alternated repeating 'yes, yes, yes… no, no, no'.

Another aspect I wish to speak to you about is the great admiration Joseph Beuys had for Ignatius of Loyola's model of spiritual discipline, a subject that has been explored at length by Father Mennekes. This was a model of discipline that the artist shared, although in his case the commitment was to the idea of creating a new society.

In this regard, the evolution of his work is seen in relation to his participation in various editions of the documenta, the most important and most international art exhibition in the world. In his first documenta participation, in 1964, he exhibited a relief and a few drawings. In the second, in 1968, he exhibited an energy-charged space which threw off electric sparks.[2] In the third documenta, which I curated in 1972, he did not show a work of art, but rather kept an office open for a hundred days, which was called the *Office for Direct Democracy by Referendum*; this was, indeed, a challenge to political parties. Naturally, this is an anarchist idea, that man might represent himself, that he is mature. In fact, Beuys did not like to use the word 'anarchist' too much, because at that time it had a negative connotation due to the militant activity of the Baader-Meinhof Group; he referred to being 'anti-authoritarian'. At the next documenta, in 1977, he put into action the closed circuit entitled *Honeypump*, which was meant to fertilise the Free International University (FIU), which he had founded to enliven debate on problems of contemporary life. Finally, in the last documenta of his life, he took on urban administrations, taking the beauty of nature to desertic cities. This was the action of planting seven thousand oak trees in Kassel, *7000 Oaks*.

We have experienced this as well at the end of the action, in the Hall of Spiritual Exercises, when Father Mennekes read his text, and then suddenly Henning Christiansen came in, interrupting him with a sound poem and music composed of noises. I think this worked well, as it demonstrated that Beuys cannot be read from a set fixed

2. This was *Fond II*, a 1968 sculpture with two copper tables charged at 20,000 volts, along with batteries and devices used in Element 1 and Element 2 of Beuys's MANRESA action.

point of his own evolution. In Madrid, for example, the sculpture called *Double Fond* was shown, a piece that Beuys did from 1954 to 1974.[3] In the piece we can clearly see that the form on the ground had been part of a crucifix, which encompasses the concept of Christ, of liberation through Christ as he sacrificed himself for us – although we do not always have to empathise with this sacrifice, taking it rather as a model that has taught us to be responsible for our own actions. That is, Christ as initial existentialism, to express it in such a way. This piece employs shapes from Beuys's earliest work[4] that are difficult to define, putting them on the floor. Thus, they continue to involve the artist being attentive to his time, turning the colours of the cross into a sculpture lying on the ground, to which an antenna rising upwards was attached. It has a spiritual quality, which includes both the emitter and the receiver, while a grounding plate is added to it. In this way it connects two energies, namely his studies into Christology and a new concept of energy.

The work *Ground* (1980-1981) is a fine example of this energy machine, and at the same time of the great freedom he made it with. The right angle was for him a symbol of thought, and in this case it is present through these copper plates, which expand it, as they contain the concept of warmth that Beuys always sought to introduce in his works. When these copper pieces arrived at the gallery wrapped in boxes of medieval wood, piled up in front of objects produced industrially, in that very moment he said 'leave it all the way it is'. In this way he had two constructive forms: one ancient, the other pertaining to new industry. In front of these copper elements – and we know that copper has the second-best electrical conductivity – he placed office furniture to introduce this call, this invitation to everyone. Most people work nowadays in the tertiary sector, seated in front of desks, seeking to invite us to develop our creativity in the office, as there too we are able to

3. The Joseph Beuys retrospective was curated by Harald Szeemann at the Museo Nacional Centro de Arte Reina Sofía, Madrid, March-June 1994.

4. Beuys began his career as a sculptor of religious images and funerary imagery.

realise ourselves as human beings. This sculpture does not respond solely to aesthetic motives, as it is complemented by different objects, such as the steel table, the chair and the cabinet; and then, to one side, he has posted *Appeal for an Alternative*, which is his most important theoretical document. In it he says that he is in favour of a third way, against communism, against capitalism, a third way that begins with the concept of human freedom. It is clear that for him the idea of freedom is first of all self-realisation, yet the second step is naturally to think of how this individual freedom, this energy, might be productive in the collective.

*

During the exhibition in Madrid, a Spanish writer viciously criticised Beuys.[5] I believe that it was like this before, that great personalities like Beuys automatically gave rise to polarised opinions, because that is exactly what he was looking for: the polarisation of Beuys was a way to awaken the spirits. Thus while some thought he was a charlatan, others felt he was a beast, in the good sense of the term, and amongst these latter we find ourselves, who considered he was a giant.

*

In *Ground*, the artist combines visual manifestation with the idea of found material, as we know it from Duchamp and others. Beuys was a loquacious person, he spoke a lot, but in this image we see a non-verbal irradiation of Beuys, as sculptor and visual artist. It recalls this same piece *Ground* shown in an enormous gallery, surrounded by works of his contemporaries, as well as sculptures by Richard Long, Mario Merz, Serra, Rückriem, Rabinowitch, Flavin, Naumann, all to a degree illuminated by the Beuys piece. He called

5. This refers to the article by Antonio Muñoz Molina, 'El descrédito del guru', published in *El País* on 30 March 1994.

this source of energy *Ground*, a term that refers to the background, first reason, ground or foundation, at the same time playing with the Dutch term 'grond', meaning earth. This presentation of *Ground* demonstrates the power of Beuys's work, which does not need words to express itself, as it has taken advantage of actionism, taking on sculptural form.

*

In closing I will speak to you of *The End of the 20th Century*, from 1983. In this sculpture we find a reactivating will, as each of these stones making up the piece can be moved, each with the size of a man; they are made of basalt, a stone of volcanic origin. Beuys has assigned each stone an organ the size of a plant pot, in this way including nature into the sculpture. Now the shared existence of these forms, which also recall prehistoric fish, is like an aquarium where we do not know whether we are looking at dead stones or living beings that have been temporarily petrified. This urge to retain the stones, which for us are like inanimate beings, is what expresses this potential sense of resurgence to us. This composition referenced the end of the twentieth century. Allow me here to conclude this exposition with a prophecy that he himself expressed: 'it depends on us to do something with these stones, which are like life, as otherwise they would be sitting around dead here, like stones.' This makes it possible to express the poetic dimension of this artist, as well as his prophetic side.

Edition
Pilar Parcerisas
Editorial Tenov

Translation
Lucy Jones - Transfiction
Jacob Daniel Schneider
Jeffrey Swartz

Correction and proofreading
Gallina Green - Trend translations
Jeffrey Swartz

Graphic design and layout
Bendita Gloria

Preprinting
Xavier Tulleuda

Printing and binding
Agpograf

Front cover image: Henning Christiansen and Bjørn Nørgaard during the action *Manresa Hbf*, 4 November 1994. ▸ Courtesy of the Arxiu Comarcal del Bages. Photo: Joan-Esteve Guillaumet.

ISBN: 978–84–944234–9–9
DL: B 4990–2022

The paper used in this publication is FSC® (Forest Stewardship Council®) certified, indicating that it comes from sustainable forests and that all the supply chain is managed responsibly.

FSC
www.fsc.org
MIX
Paper from responsible sources
FSC® C104592

Acknowledgments
The editors wish to express their gratitude to the institutions and people who have contributed to the conception and realisation of this book.

Pilar Parcerisas wishes to express her gratitude to all the people who contributed to the *Manresa Hbf* action (1994):

Valentí Roqueta Guillamet (Former president, Fundació Caixa Manresa), Jaume Torras Rodergas (Former director, Fundació Caixa Manresa), and the production team: Montse Badia, Josep Duocastella, Abdó Martí and Francesc Parcerisas.

This book has been published with the support of:

Generalitat de Catalunya
Departament de Cultura

Institut Català de les Empreses Culturals

Ajuntament de Manresa

Manresa 2022 Transforma

EMBASSY OF DENMARK
Madrid

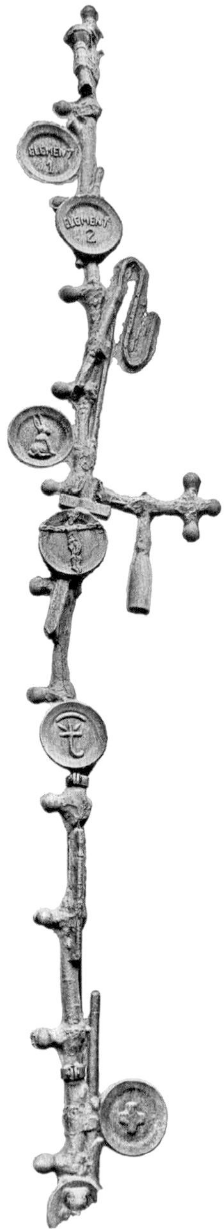
ELEMENT 1
ELEMENT 2